PAUL GATER'S
GHOST REPORTER – *The Files*

- 10 YEARS OF INVESTIGATING THE SUPERNATURAL

This is Paul's fourth 'ghost book', following his successful *LIVING WITH GHOSTS, GHOSTS AT WAR* and *THE SECRET LIVES OF GHOSTS*

- Sections include

THE UNDERWORLD; THE MYSTERIOUS UNIVERSE; HAUNTED GROUND; GOING HOME.

- 30 'SUPERNATURAL SNIPPETS'

Amazing stories of everything from **Aliens** *to* **Zoological Monsters**. *All kinds of* **Ghosts, Hauntings** *&* **Mysterious Phenomena** *in between. Also* **Personal Encounters** *with* **The Unknown.**

'his best yet!' – Danae Slenko, Mystic Motes

1

Books by Paul Gater

Living with Ghosts
Ghosts at War
The Secret Lives of Ghosts

The Magic of Flowers

GHOST REPORTER
The Files

Paul Gater

An Anecdotes Book

CONTENTS

SUPERNATURAL SNIPPETS No 2
The Mysterious Universe

PART THREE - HAUNTED GROUND

SUPERNATURAL SNIPPETS No 3
Haunted Ground

PART FOUR - GOING HOME

Acknowledgements

This book explores many areas I have not covered before. And though I say 'I', various people have contributed their company, encouragement and support, as well as sharing their expertise in a wide range of paranormal fields. Thanks and acknowledgement to them all, especially my wife Dilys Gater, a psychic medium and author of many spiritual books.

Thanks also to Helen Sanchez de la Nuez who has been with us on several occasions mentioned in the book, for her interest and her unique and stimulating company; Tarot Reader Jaine Francis, together with Helen and another good friend Hugh Robertson Black, has contributed valuable material and much appreciated on-going support over time.

Paul Gater

Acknowledgements are made to the following newspapers and magazines where my work has appeared: *Your Leek Paper, The Leek Post & Times, The Moorlands Trader, The Staffordshire Evening Sentinel, Around Leek & Staffordshire Moorlands Magazine, Local Life Magazine (Cheshire), Prediction* and *Psychic News*. Also *BBC Radio Stoke, Signal Radio, Moorlands Radio, BBC West Midlands, BBC Three Counties* and *BBC Northampton* for their keen interest.

INTRODUCTION

I have spent the last ten years researching and reporting on supernatural phenomena both specifically ghostly and supernatural in general – you could say, from Aliens to Zoological phantom beings, from ghostly to ghastly. As a chronicler of the 'Strange to Tell' I have recorded the results of my research via regular newspaper columns and magazine articles, as well as four books.

Although vaguely aware of ghosts and strange 'goings-on' since childhood, it was only after a career working in horticulture, close to the natural world, that my first serious investigations into the unpredictable and the supernatural were undertaken and resulted in my first 'ghost' book - *Living with Ghosts*. This was a completely new departure for me, for though I had always aspired (with some success) to be a writer, my previous fields had been poetry and playwriting: investigating the supernatural meant entering a new dimension and learning to accept the unbelievable, the result partly of having interviewed such a lot of people who had daily connections with properties that were 'active'. I was amazed at the number of occupants of those properties who readily acknowledged the fact, and shared their lives as normally as possible with one, two or more presences from different periods of history in the house. Even more amazing was the fact that often, the same people would insist forcefully that they did not believe in ghosts!

My investigative book was favourably received by the critics and I found myself being interviewed in the press and on a number of radio stations, including a phone-in for BBC WM at midnight – 'the Witching Hour'!

From then on, I was hooked and have been on innumerable investigations in the years since, visiting strange, eerie places, attending psychic events and, as always, talking to people who wanted to share their unusual experiences – in the street, at Craft and Psychic fairs or indeed, anywhere. Individuals who have had paranormal experiences - whether just one memorable episode or many, eagerly wanted to tell me about them. And as a result of personal evidence gained as well as on-going research, I began to discover a great deal about the strange, mysterious worlds that interact with our own.

My second ghost book *Ghosts at War* dealt with the many supernatural aspects of conflict, including haunted battlefields, ghostly armies, weapons, phantom ships and planes, as well as individual revenants. I discovered that some battles (in ancient and modern times) have been seen in ghostly re-play both on the ground and in the sky, whether partially or completely, sometimes visually, sometimes only with sound effects. Since I live on the border between the Peak District and the Staffordshire Moorlands, I was particularly interested to hear that when Bonnie Prince Charlie and his Scottish army passed through the Staffordshire-Derbyshire area in 1745 on his way south, he left behind him a ghostly trail: besides eerie and frightening atmospheres being sensed in the area, dishevelled, kilted ghostly soldiers have been seen, some with their own individual tales of violence and tragedy. Though the Prince himself reputedly knocked on the door of the Vicarage in the local market town of Leek, requesting shelter, there seem to be no reports of a royal ghostly presence, though victims of violence continue to haunt these wild, still remote places. Many ghostly soldiers – as far back as the Romans as well as up to the present day - continue to appear in relevant locations.

In 2013 my third book, *The Secret Lives of Ghosts*, was published. This is an exploration into how the phantoms which haunt our countryside and towns live busy, passionate lives filled with as much intrigue and emotion as they did when physically here on earth. Again I included a large number of strange-but-true 'ghost stories' and various editions of my books – including Large Print –

are now read all over the world. It was this wealth of material, recently re-discovered when I was browsing through my collection of stories and events that had appeared in my media articles but not yet in book form, that resulted in *Ghost Reporter – the Files*. A wide-ranging selection is also included here of my best *'Supernatural Snippets'* taken from various newspapers and journals, some which have appeared on-line over the last 4 years on the website: leekonline.co.uk.

EXPLORING THE THRESHOLD

(Recorded 14th November, 2012)
(Discussion on Dilys's book **To Fields of Gold***)*

The following report taken from an interview with Dilys and Helen, provides some information on mediumship and gives an idea of the stimulating discussions which have helped to shape my thoughts.

Helen: I thought it was such a thorough compilation of your experiences as a medium, Dilys, backed up by the kudos of quotations from artists and philosophers – very intuitive people who obviously felt close to the edge of the threshold between life and death themselves. And because you had also quoted from your own additional books, that added extra weight to the whole thing.

Dilys: As an actor, Helen, and perhaps you could say, as a novice who is interested in the spiritual, what did you think about the information in the book on how to develop and how to reach the boundaries.

Helen: I have taught English, I read a lot of poetry and philosophy. I see a lot of drama and I'm involved in its presentation, which besides being the story is also a search for the meaning of life.

Dilys: Although I've met a lot of actors, performers and singers, they are all attempting to reach the threshold -

Helen: - yes, and explain this meaning of life. That's what it is all about. It always takes writers and artists – creative people – to express, to explain – something they find hard to define. Something that can't be expressed in words. You have to do it emotionally. For instance, by way of drama, like in a Pinter play, in his pauses. He said more by silence than by means of the word. Also, the actors of the play contribute by the way they look and their body language. Whereas in real life, you can usually tell by looking at someone, their expression and the way they move.

Dilys: I mention body language in my books. Regarding mediumship, I deliberately avoid looking at my sitters because I don't want to see their body language. I know that the truth is something far beyond that – something that comes out, often amazingly different.

Helen: There again, that sitter may be grasping into the void. Or they're trying to cover up. It is important to follow your instinct, or intuition. You may go against your instincts because you think you're wrong -

Dilys: Like in mediumship. It rarely comes as a certainty. It might come as certainty to you (the medium), but it's very difficult to trust that certainty when it goes in the face of everything you have been told.

Helen: At work, for example, there was somebody I didn't like. But I couldn't help it. I felt she was the sort who'd stab you in the back. Yet I wondered if I was being too severe in my opinion of her. Subsequently, however, I found I'd been quite right. She'd put on this face and everyone else had thought she was marvellous.

Dilys: It was probably what you had sensed through your own developing 'second sight'. It's very difficult for the beginner – even for the more experienced. It was difficult for me when, for example, I found an elemental spirit crouched on Doreen's hearthrug in front of the fire (*one of the cases discussed in my book*). There I was standing with my crucifix and holy water, pushing my foot into the freezing cold against this 'thing' that wasn't visible to anyone else, trying to edge it away towards the door. I thought I must have looked like a maniac! 'This can't be true!' I often say to myself. I've even found it difficult sometimes to say prayers in the classes I take, at the end of the evening or a meeting. I've felt as though I was acting a part. It's just practice and experience though; my students expect me to do it and it helps them as it helps me.

But there's always this 'thing' of doubt that comes and says over my shoulder: 'Who do you think you are?'

Helen: But because you're very sensitive you don't want to hurt other people.

Dilys: And you can pick up on how you could hurt them. Many a time, I've been asked by a client about the child they're expecting - 'the baby'. I've looked at the tarot cards and have seen that they're going to lose that baby, or they're not going to have one at all. You can never say that though because you might be wrong. Some readers do, they see it and they say it. But one of the few certainties about interpreting the cards is that there is such a lot that people can do to change themselves. They can change their fate through their own free will. Sometimes I think they can read my mind when I look at the cards and 'see' something negative, so I keep a blank face and reassure them: 'Yes, you'll have a child, etc etc, despite a few blips.'

Helen: Yes, you're right. People *can* change their fate, but they often don't know how to.

PART ONE
THE UNDERWORLD

1 GHOST HUNTER, GHOST WRITER

I would describe myself as an investigator, journalist and storyteller with an ever-developing perception of 'things' that are slightly (or indeed, sometimes very far) beyond the norm. I recognised this initially as a keen sense of appreciation for the countryside, animals, flowers and trees – something which in fact, I still possess. And although I embarked on a career in horticulture and have spent my working life very close to the natural world, I also sensed the presence of some other dimension – that of the paranormal – even from childhood.

At one time, I maintained gardens for a number of my clients. My first fully-knowing encounter with those other dimensions began to occur regularly when I was asked to restore the neglected grounds of a large 1930s property to their former splendour. One afternoon I became aware of a man – identified later from old photographs as the original owner - watching me keenly from a terrace that ran along the rear of the house as I worked on the run-down rock garden below. This continued over several months. I knew, of course, that he was deceased, and he always vanished whenever I returned his look, but there was a relaxed, happy atmosphere about the place. His last appearance was on the day I completed the restoration, when he stared at me for a long moment, half-smiling, then vanished and I did not see him again.

Interestingly, when I told my mother about these encounters, she expressed amazement, having little belief in ghosts. Yet shortly after she died, I 'saw' her too. It was in the lounge of the family home one evening when I walked into the dark room from the hall. In the light slanting through the door, I saw her familiar image. Characteristically, she was busily checking the quality of some new curtains that had recently been hung at the bay windows. 'Hello!' I said, without thinking. 'What are *you* doing here?' And at that, she disappeared.

That family home had an entity of its own, similar in some ways to other disturbed properties I would later visit with Dilys. I discovered that many 'haunted houses' display no obvious signs of supernatural activity, no Grey Ladies, shrouded figures or clanking chains. Genuine hauntings can be far subtler. The atmosphere in the family home at times felt strange and physically out of proportion. For example, walking across the front room seemed to be a much greater distance than it actually was. Meanwhile, the steps of the staircase appeared to go on a very long way – so much so that, looking out of a normal first-floor window, you had the impression of being three floors up! Once I had started to explore the supernatural I learned to quickly pick up on atmospheres as a result – even in other people's houses.

Yet in this setting my brother and I had been happily brought up and from an early age I was very aware of the magic of the garden and the beauty of its flowers – my memories of those sunlit childhood days seemingly flourishing under constant blue skies helped to inspire another of my books – *The Magic of Flowers*. Though not about ghosts, this does mention the other-worldly powers and lore of flowers.

Apart from school-work, socialising with friends and later the usual activities of a teenager, I was learning my craft as a horticulturist, getting my hands dirty, planting trees and shrubs (sometimes with help from my father before I left home to attend Pershore College of Horticulture). As a potential writer I wrote poetry, plays and some early articles which I was lucky enough to have published in *Fur and Feather*, *Amateur Gardening* and *Popular Gardening*. One of my subjects was 'Livestock Row' – a small shed and several hutches and pens that housed a number of rabbits and guinea-pigs – and two tortoises. An aquarium each of goldfish and tropical fish resided in the conservatory, while a cage in the living-room was home to a pair of boisterous budgerigars. Everyday contact with the animals – from feeding, cleaning them out, to holding and gently stroking them – taught me to appreciate the dignity and spirituality of all animals, something again I sensed in my work.

But the enquiring mind of the ghost hunter must have been already there in embryo. I had listened to a plethora of strange village tales, particularly those told by the older residents, of an age long past, and had also frequently wandered through nearby fields and the very atmospheric woods, settings to some of those old stories which greatly influenced me. I was widely-read on such matters, having absorbed amongst other things, the gripping tales of Edgar Allan Poe and a volume of Thomas Hardy's powerful short stories. My interest in the supernatural was keen, with a definite awareness of an alternative world running parallel with our own, with hardly a veil between. I felt fully equipped for any chance encounter with any kind of spirit.

So I spent my career as a horticulturist, working in Worcestershire, Warwickshire and South Staffordshire; later I returned to my family home near Newcastle-under-Lyme, spending some years at the famous Trentham Gardens. Eventually I built up a small garden maintenance business, which I was still running when I began to investigate the paranormal, as a result of Dilys (whom I had previously known when she lived in Stoke-on-Trent) arriving from London to share the family home, where I was by this time living on my own.

Over the next few years Dilys, a psychic medium, investigated the possible reasons why the house seemed to be so 'out-of-focus' and possess such a strange, sometimes oppressive atmosphere. This, I learned, was not necessarily because of a ghostly presence, but due to a high degree of negativity – 'dark energy' - rising from the ground beneath, possibly caused by an underground stream, stagnant water or metals present very deep down in the earth. There were also coal mining galleries beneath the road; such phenomena can have an effect on people living in the house, making them feel inexplicably unwell, as if passing from crisis to crisis, which I had experienced myself from time to time, especially in my adult years.

Dilys also identified a nearby plot of land that to her exuded great sadness and suffering, the atmosphere at times stultifying, a scene of death and destruction – maybe even of plague. Psychically, she saw what seemed like smoke, burning debris and holes in the ground, reminiscent of old photographs of the First World War of woods and fields having been blown into oblivion. Later I recollected my parents telling me when I was about 14 that they had been told the land in question was once a smallholding. Swine fever had struck some time during the 1920s and after being slaughtered, the bodies of the pigs were burned where they lay, and their remains buried.

Eventually, Dilys and I moved to live in the market town of Leek in the Staffordshire Moorlands. This, we discovered, is an extremely spiritual and psychic area and here I was introduced by experts to the disciplines of clairvoyance, dowsing, healing, mediumship, the Tarot and psychic investigation. An atmospheric and spiritual place as well as a tourist centre, Leek also has a proud history as an affluent industrial mill-town, with connections to William Morris, Edward Burne-Jones – even Oscar Wilde! It has played a significant part in history, and I particularly researched the year 1745, when Bonnie Prince Charlie and his Scottish army passed through on their way south, hoping to wrest the Crown from the head of George II. I have mentioned that the Prince's army had left many gruesome legends and ghostly echoes behind.

There are many dark tales and events continuing to cast their shadows over the brightness of the living. I discovered that the atmospheres in places such as Bronze Age burial sites, plague pits, churchyards, castles, or dungeons – sites of trauma, fear, suspicion and secrecy - can hold their intensity for a long time, sometimes for centuries afterwards. Similarly, the places where animals have been slaughtered can also be sensed to hold strong atmospheres; not only on the sites of old abattoirs, but farm buildings and areas behind old cottages where 'unofficial' killings used to take place. The atmosphere along old drovers' roads and tracks may be permeated by the feelings of the animals sensing they were being taken for slaughter. Past sensations of pain and fear, as well as hate, revenge and acts of cruelty are what lie behind a good deal of the hauntings still perpetuated in the present.

Thanks to the great friendliness of the people of Leek and their willingness to share stories and experiences of other world activities, both Dilys and I found residence there conducive to our work. (Incidentally, it was also in Leek that we got married). She carried out consultations and healing; I accompanied her to various properties to assess the different types of spiritual presences and organised Psychic Fairs. In due course we were invited to give talks at the Green Dragon Earth Mysteries Society, a monthly 'get-together' for like-minded people. I was invited to contribute regular columns on 'strange tales' for local papers; in 2003, as a result of my research into the paranormal, my first book *Living with Ghosts,* came to be published, appearing both here and in the United States, and also in Large Print editions.

I discovered I was now living in a very potent area that also took in Derbyshire, with its ancient knowledge and beliefs that once held sway for hundreds of years. As a link between now and then, the Bronze Age circle of stones on Stanton Moor, known as The Nine Ladies, is connected nowadays to modern witchcraft and pagan celebrations – a partly exposed, magical place which I was to visit; I found the Derbyshire Peaks cunningly concealed a honeycombed underworld of mysterious caves, old haunted mines, underground caverns, some dry with others being massively flooded by what our ancestors referred to as the River Styx, 'River of the Dead'.

This same world teems with supernatural activity and presences from other dimensions. Below Topley Pike, four miles west of Bakewell, is Deepdale Cave, also known as Thirst House, an abbreviation of Hob o' the Hurst's House; Hurst meaning 'a wooded place'. Here there once lived a very tiny elf, or hob, guardian of a nearby spring. One evening, a farmer on his way home to Chelmorten, caught the hob and put it into his bag. The tiny being, however, did little else but cry and shriek – so much so that the farmer released it, and it quickly returned to the security of its cave. With water being one of the creative elements of life, believers in the Fairy Realm say that the magical presence of the small being once made it possible for the spring water to cure every disease known to man – provided it was drunk on Good Friday.

Another Derbyshire cave is that of Beeley, similarly known as Hob o' the Hurst's House, outside the village of Beeley, near to Chatsworth. Defined as a round Bronze Age (1600-1000 BC) barrow burial mound, it is actually square-shaped, about 10m (eleven yards) across, with surrounding bank and ditch. An excavation by Thomas Bateman in the mid-1800s revealed a stone-lined grave in which a body had been cremated. As with many other burial places in Derbyshire, the local population believed it to be the home of the goblin, Hob Hurst. If Hob felt in a good mood, farmers of the area would expect a good harvest and the cows to yield plenty of milk. However, if harvests were poor and the cows 'dried up', they knew that Hob was in a bad mood.

I have never knowingly encountered fairies, goblins or elves during my investigations but I did interview a former soldier who regularly encountered the flower fairies in the garden he and his wife had much pleasure in cultivating. This very tough man generously shared his experiences with me when I was working on *The Magic of Flowers*, telling me that he had been aware of the 'small folk' since the age of eleven.

One of my most memorable psychic experiences occurred when Dilys and I were invited to supper by the new owner of 'the most haunted cottage' in Britain, a grey sandstone, three-storied 19th century building situated in a village near to Ashbourne. Its sale had been widely covered by the media, and it was pure coincidence that the owner had come to Leek for a Tarot consultation with Dilys. We kept in touch for several years, visiting the property on many occasions. It was the first 'case' I discussed in the opening chapter of *Living with Ghosts*, where I narrated its story and interviewed the owner.

The house had a genuinely horrific reputation. Dilys, as a psychic medium, was able to clarify the complicated situation within, informing our host of a number of entities present as well as situations (as with my own family home) occurring in the garden and surrounding area – these included the sites of an ancient burial ground, former gallows tree and Methodist Chapel. She felt that the resident spirits (or at least, one of them) regarded our presence as a possible threat, and during one of our candle-lit meals I became aware at one point of the walls silently pulsating, gradually moving in on us, out of focus, a sensation similar to that of migraine. After the pressure had been applied, it slowly receded, leaving a mental sense of exhaustion behind – Dilys experienced this to such a degree that it took her several days to 'cleanse' herself of the effects after each visit; I also 'saw' another of the entities in the house. She was never asked by the owner to move the 'presences' on, nor did she offer to do so – and she felt they consequently, though grudgingly, respected her for it. These were actively defensive presences that had even resisted blessings carried out on several occasions on the property by the Church.

I have written elsewhere about these events in greater detail, but mention them here to underline the fact that the paranormal has its own set of rules which, to us, may seem strange and mystifying, even terrifying at times.

As time passed and my book became known, I found that complete strangers were stopping me in the street or at Craft Fairs we attended in the Derbyshire village of Hartington, to tell me their intriguing stories – which I wrote down immediately afterwards, to retain the 'voices' of the individual tellers. And although Dilys and I had moved to Buxton by the time I wrote my next book *Ghosts at War,* it was the iconic Nicholson War Memorial in Leek that originally gave me the idea for the subject.

Working on *Living with Ghosts* involved interviews with a large number of people. Although I naturally relied also on personal experiences where possible, when working on a book, *Ghosts at War* also necessitated much research; it was essential to access more than one source of information about a particular happening, in order to arrive at a personal opinion. My mind was cast back to when I was living in Worcestershire as a student, and encountering some veterans from World War One. Having survived its horrors, they were beings who – even after more than forty years – still seemed haunted by the ghosts within, speaking little of their past ordeals.

There were three former German prisoners from World War Two, working at the same market-garden as myself. They had remained in the United Kingdom when hostilities ceased and had eventually married local girls. After all, as one of them said, by 1945, there was nothing left of their home country but 'rubble and the ghosts'. Although aged twenty, I felt I understood; their own ghosts perhaps came looking over my shoulder years later, when I came to write *Ghosts at War.*

2 THE DARK SIDE

As part of a group guided by someone ahead of us with a lamp, Dilys and I cautiously made our way through a narrow passage far below ground. Suddenly, a lighting-system automatically switched on as the passage dissolved into a long, high-ceilinged gallery. Walking along one side, we looked across to the opposite wall of rock and were surprised to see that a broad stretch of earth had been hollowed out in a number of places as if by some large animal. Our guide told us that this was where wild bears hibernated during the winters of over one thousand years ago.

Seeing the hollows so well preserved, as though the animals had just gone outside, gave me the feeling that although the bears were truly no longer there physically, spiritually they were still very much around and that we visitors were intruders in their winter quarters. It didn't matter that a thousand years or so stood between them and ourselves. To me, rocks and caves represent time and distance, yet in themselves are able to manipulate both time and distance according to certain aspects of the human mind. Our visit to the Aillwyce Bear Caves was the culmination of a memorable stay in the West of Ireland that Dilys and I undertook a few years ago.

Encountering a cave, whether in woodland or amid rocky terrain, can still produce a sense of awe, wonder and even a degree of hesitation in us even today. To our ancestors it would have been even more deeply significant, with their ingrained reverence towards Nature and towards the mysteries far beyond. To them, a cave offered refuge not only to the wild beasts that no longer threaten us (like wolves and bears), but also to many strange, supernatural entities. Even the Celtic Druids were aware of those unseen worlds that interact with the visible; and where our ancestors challenged those beasts and sought shelter for themselves, their fearful belief in supernatural entities was likely to have persisted nonetheless. For caves represented an entrance to what the Celts would have referred to as Annwn (the 'Loveless Region'), regarded over the centuries as 'demonic and evil' – the Underworld – ruled by forces far beyond their control.

To most people the Underworld represents a 'Hell', a place where sinners are dispatched to suffer for their wrong-doings. Hell is well represented in tradition and literature, as well as in religious belief. It was to here that, for his sins, Don Giovanni, the serial womaniser in Mozart's opera of that name, was finally cast down into the flames.

So to the ancients, the Underworld was a real, an actual place – people went there but often returned to walk the earth again. During my research, I found that various cultures had differing views about the Underworld, though the idea of the soul travelling across a river, or tackling some sort of watery obstacle to get to such a domain 'below ground' has been the subject of many traditions. According to songs and spirituals, crossing the River Jordan was essential in order to arrive at the Promised Land. In Greek mythology, the souls of the dead were ferried by the boatman Charon, across the River Styx. When he was dying, the legendary King Arthur was taken by barge to the Isle of Avalon. The Vikings would set a departed warrior's ship alight with his body on board, thus beginning his voyage to the Underworld. The old Norse word for boat, 'ludr', also meant both coffin and cradle, the shamanic vision showing death and rebirth to be the same. In various cultures, when the departed soul was taken over the water, there would have been coins placed on the eyes or in the mouth, in order to pay the ferryman for his services. A lot of effort was put into making sure that the deceased person was taken across the River Styx and the subject, in one form or another, has tended to attract the attention of various creative artists. It was after seeing a black and white print of a painting by Arnold Bocklin that

Sergei Rachmaninov composed his atmospheric orchestral poem *The Isle of the Dead*, portraying the Boatman of Death as he conveys a departed soul on the unremitting journey from one dimension to the other.

Until comparatively recently in terms of human history, conditions were likely to be very dark and uncertain so far as daily life in all its aspects was concerned - religiously, politically and militarily. The elements themselves helped to foster widespread fear and belief in ghosts, spirits, fairies and further supernatural elements. After sunset – particularly during the long winter months – there was little, if any, natural lighting except the moon; this in itself was a proven formula for promoting belief in the supernatural. Moonlight revealed a dangerous dimension - unrecognised shadows of people were seen, weird forms moved stealthily through the dimly-lit streets of a town, hedges assumed strange shapes in the vision of someone walking along a country lane at dusk, the echo of one's own footsteps or the call of an owl or night animal – all these would easily have fed the vulnerable imagination.

I have heard and researched many tales about the terrors of the Underworld. The Staffordshire/ Derbyshire border where I live is particularly rich in them, especially since it is so wild – the huge expanses of moorland and grim rocky outcrops are just the setting for scary tales. Though ghosts may haunt town houses or streets, it appears that the Underworld as such does not seem to figure so much in tales of urban life.

Eldon Hole, just north of Peak Forest village was once believed to be the 'Devil's Bolt-hole' to Hell. Years ago, a goose belonging to an old woman of the locality is said to have fallen down the hole, only to emerge three days later from the famous Peak Cavern, two miles away – interestingly, with its feathers singed! During the 1500s the Earl of Leicester, hoping to discover the true depth of Eldon Hole, had a local man lowered down by rope. Eventually, when he was pulled up, it was found he had lost consciousness and he died soon afterwards. Local gossip declared that he must have come face-to-face with none other than 'Auld Horney' himself, an alternative name for the Devil.

Years later, another man was lowered down on a rope reputedly over a mile in length, but it still did not reach the bottom; while during the 18th century, it is said that two highwaymen forced one of their victims to step over the edge 'into Eternity'. Meanwhile, a Fellow of the Royal Society independently discovered that the Devil's Bolt-hole to Hell was approximately 55m (180 feet) in depth, though how he arrived at this result was not revealed.

So here lies a dark, murky world, a challenging environment where narrow passages and secret chambers echo to flowing water – from the merest trickle to a thunderous, swirling force roaring its way down to a dreadful eternity, capable even of overwhelming the flames of Hell. (Or might the latter be more than capable of reducing such a force to a constant hiss of steam?)

Whether a believer in the world of the supernatural or not, who can fail to be gripped by tales of the sleepless dead, the return of individuals interred alive in ancient burial chambers, the tormented souls who walk the earth consumed by guilt, jealousy, revenge or remorse, the subject of 'true' tales as well as those narrated by masters of ghoulish horror like M.R. James, Edith Nesbit or H.P. Lovecraft. Our ancestors feared caves as places likely to be occupied by supernatural entities, and in the same way dreaded places where the dead are interred. So we can often feel very uneasy if entering old, overgrown burial grounds; and superstitions cling to standing stones that denote a sacred place – possibly a resting place - set in a Celtic landscape. Do the departed rest peacefully? If not, why? Do spirits linger because they were happy or unhappy? Because they died violently? Because some of their concerns in life have been left unfinished? All these are matters for the enquiring mind of any ghost-reporter.

Boudicca, the great warrior Queen of the Iceni, is famous for her military struggles with the Roman overlords who occupied Britain. After her army had been involved in several ruthless campaigns against the occupying forces, it was heavily defeated by the Roman Governor Suetonius Paulinus in 62 AD somewhere in southern England, the exact location unspecified by Tacitus, the Roman historian. To escape capture, Boudicca and her two daughters chose the only way out – the Roman way – by suicide.

Generations have since speculated over the site of her final resting-place. Some believe it could be under what is now King's Cross, one of London's busiest railway stations, or in Parliament Fields; two other possible locations are Quidenham and Garboldisham Heath in Norfolk. However, it is also believed that Boudicca was a Druid, a member of the Celtic spiritual hierarchy whose base was on the island of Mona (Anglesey); tradition has it that after her death, her body was secretly transported north, up through the Welsh Marches, for burial on Mona's mystic isle. Echoes of that epic journey are said to resonate to this day. During her own research Dilys spoke to people living alongside the Old Route, who had occasionally heard the frantic galloping of horses and the grinding of phantom chariot wheels in the dead of night as the funeral group passed, guarded by those faithful to their Druid beliefs. On discovering that Mona was now occupied by the Romans and that the sacred groves had been destroyed, Boudicca's followers are said to have buried her somewhere secretly on the mainland, possibly in an ancient burial chamber such as the one on Gop Carn, at Gwaenysgor in North Wales (though this is unproved).

For many, despite its hint of the Underworld, that might have been the end of a well-known story, despite its veil of mystery. But the ghostly Warrior Queen has additionally been seen by villagers at Cammeringham in Lincolnshire – her long, red hair billowing as she stands upright, cracking her whip above the backs of the two horses pulling her chariot on some phantom mission. She and the spirits of her two daughters have also appeared in the area around the old earthworks at Ambresbury, where it is believed the three of them poisoned themselves. No doubt Boudicca would have preferred to rest on the sacred isle of Mona; being a queen, she deserved something better than being lost in an anonymous grave. Despite having been vanquished, her name - 'Boudicca' – ironically means 'victory'; and significantly, it is she and her story which passed into popular legend, whereas the name of the Roman Governor of Britain, Suetonius Paulinus, has been largely forgotten.

There are other indications that the dead continue their earthly struggles in phantom form. The remains of several megaliths on Blue Bell Hill, in Kent, indicate a number of prehistoric burial chambers: one known as Kit's Coty House is believed to be the final resting-place of a British chieftain who was killed in a fight with the Jutish leader, Horsa in 455 AD. But do the warriors rest in peace? According to witnesses, the combatants are occasionally seen re-enacting their struggle to the death, but in complete silence.

Perhaps the most notorious graveyard, spirit-wise, is Boot Hill Graveyard in Tombstone, Arizona. Most of its 250 dead occupants actually did 'die with their boots on', confirming the area's violent past, particularly during the period 1878-1884. During this time it became the final resting-place for all sorts of outlaws, hoodlums, fraudsters, gold prospectors and 'ladies of virtue'. It also accommodates those gunmen who fell during the legendary gunfight of the O.K. Corral. It is not surprising that the place is reputed to seethe with an atmosphere of meanness, enmity and shame that can be 'picked up' by sensitive visitors. Strange lights have been seen and inexplicable noises heard, indicating the restlessness of souls forever arising nightly (or even daily) to try and complete their unfinished business. Many visitors at the site are reported as having taken photographs and been amazed when figures not visible at the time appeared on their prints after the films were developed.

During the 1940s the place was given a glamorous 'makeover', enabling Boot Hill to become a great stop-off destination for tourists. And with blue skies, bathed in sunshine, this – like the majority of burial plots – can seem a peaceful resting-place. However, the West was notoriously wild, and the phantom occupants here were tough guys not likely to 'rest in peace'.

A quiet grave is something that many spirits seem to crave for if they have been denied the ritual of a traditional burial. A sad story from 11th century Holywell, in Cambridgeshire, saw a maiden named Juliet Tewsley cruelly jilted by Thomas Zoul, a woodcutter. After hanging herself as a consequence, it was Thomas who, discovering the hapless young woman, cut her down and buried her where he had found her, marking the grave with a stone slab. Years later, the Old Ferry Boat Inn was built over the site and since then, her troubled ghost has been seen not only inside the inn itself but on the bank of the nearby River Ouse. The original stone slab, now incorporated in the floor, is said to bring bad luck to anyone who sets foot on it and for the curse to be lifted, the culprit must buy a round of drinks for the house! In March every year, so it is said, the current landlord holds a huge party to honour Juliet's memory, but this maiden who was so rejected in life might well be yearning – after hundreds of years – to be allowed to rest in a peaceful churchyard rather than included in a noisy party, even if in her honour!

Below Chapel Hill, by the harbour at Polperro in Cornwall, is a cave known as Willy Willcocks' Hole. While exploring the cave, Willcocks, despite being a local fisherman, got totally lost in a maze of dark passages and it is said that his cries can still be heard, his troubled spirit desperately seeking not only that elusive way of escape, but also a desire for burial in consecrated ground.

There are probably many more restless dead who are denied that wish. Praa Sands, a coastal village in Cornwall, experienced times when ships were lured onto rocks by wreckers out to plunder their cargoes. Any survivors, including sailors, were killed and disposed of, and the despairing cries of such sad victims, buried in un-consecrated ground, have been heard on the eerie night air.

Cornwall has always been synonymous with the sea and mining. The popular resort of Portreath used to be from where tin was taken to South Wales. Ships would return with coal to fuel the steam engines used in the Cornish mines. The tradition of mining in Cornwall goes back to the Bronze Age, with a high point for tin-mining that lasted from the Middle Ages to well into the 19th century. Is it any wonder that myths, legends and superstition concerning the industry have accrued over such a stretch of time?

Not much is known of the widow Dorcas who once lived in one of the small cottages near to Polbreen Mine at St. Agnes, on the north Cornish coast. She committed suicide by throwing herself down the mineshaft shortly after her husband died in an accident at the mine. Her broken body was subsequently retrieved and buried but her spirit remained in the dark galleries below. She took perverse pleasure in calling the men from their task of mining ore and wasting their time. On one occasion, she called to one of the miners who went to investigate. Just then, a serious roof-collapse occurred at the very place where he had been working only moments before – so Dorcas had actually saved his life.

Other entities walked the dark galleries of the mines. The miners believed implicitly in the 'knockers' – elves or dwarfs whose tappings were believed to indicate a rich lode of ore deep down in the workings. It was also believed that knockers were actually spirits of the Jews who had crucified Christ, and who had to do penance in the 'Underworld' below the earth as a consequence. Described as 'thin-limbed and hook-nosed', they were usually regarded as benevolent although, amongst other things, whistling offended them. All miners knew that anyone whistling in a mine was simply inviting doom and disaster.

The presence of a local group of knockers, known as the Kobolds, is said to occupy a long disused tunnel on Bodmin Moor called 'The Roaring Shaft'. They are reputedly responsible for the numerous cracking, bangs and other mysterious sounds rising, which are believed to be a warning to everyone to keep away from imminent danger.

Other spirits also made their presences felt in the mines. At Wheal Vor, near Helston, a phantom white hare would appear just prior to an accident. At several mines a spectral hand clawing at a ladder was often seen, usually just as a miner was descending into a shaft – this was also known to be a dire warning.

At Wheal Coates, which goes down to the sea, is another mine near to St. Agnes; this place, too, is occupied by the ghosts of miners who once worked and perished amid the grimy, challenging conditions. In the Calstock area, a village in the south east of Cornwall became especially important with the discovery of copper in the late 19th century. Along one of the roads into the village, a group of phantom miners wearing old-fashioned work-clothes and carrying candles, is often seen.

Similarly at Bedruthan Steps, east of Newquay on the north Cornish coast, many locals have heard miners' boots tramping towards an old iron mine, where the invisible miners are then heard chipping away at the rock with their picks. Though often signifying disaster and lives lost in terrible circumstances, it might be reassuring that in a spiritual sense, many miners may have chosen to work happily on with their comrades as phantoms, deep in their own Underworld, which to them is a benevolent and not a threatening place.

3 THE PEAK CAVERN, DERBYSHIRE

'I perceived to the right, in the hollow of the cavern, a whole subterranean village where the inhabitants, on account of its being Sunday, were resting from their work and with happy and cheerful looks were sitting at the doors of their huts along with their children. We had scarcely passed these small subterranean houses when I perceived a number of large wheels, on which these human moles, the inhabitants of the cavern, make ropes.'

Moritz's Travels 1782

The element of earth was regarded by the Ancients as home to the Great Mother, and the Underworld below accessible through many caves and pot-holes. So on a warm, sunny day in early summer, I took the opportunity – together with Dilys and our friend Helen – to visit the amazing Peak Cavern at Castleton, in Derbyshire. Looking at the beautiful, yet dramatic landscape now, I find it hard to imagine the area having been peppered with numerous productive lead mines as it was during the 17th, 18th and 19th centuries, in which our destination had played its part.

From the centre of the village of Castleton we walked briskly along the path, flanked by fast-flowing water, up past former lead-miners' cottages, now converted into modern holiday-lets. Suddenly, we were confronted by a huge limestone gorge, with vertical cliffs rising some 250 ft in height, dull ochre in colour with trees, ferns and ivy clinging miraculously to them. A number of jackdaws, quietly cawing to each other, were flying around before disappearing high up into the crevices. They could just as well have been pterodactyls, this incredible spectacle reminiscent of Conan Doyle's story of *The Lost World*.

Water flowed out from the bottom of the cliff to our left, below the path that lead directly into the Peak Cavern, the entrance chamber, breathtaking in itself, the largest natural cave entrance in the British Isles – over 100 ft in width with a very spacious vestibule within. Entering this Temple to Subterranea, initially we experienced that same hushed reverence felt on going into a woodland or forest – that fusion of man with Nature. We joined a small group of other visitors as we awaited our guide. The floor sloped away to the left in a series of six wide steps and he pointed out that each one was a ropewalk with its (now restored) winders and pulley-poles, used for rope-making by families who had surprisingly lived (having once constructed their own dwelling-places – little more than hovels – inside the cave itself) and worked there for about three hundred years or even longer. References exist of the British Fleet that fought the Spanish Armada having used rope that had been made in the Cavern. A woman named Mary Knight, who died in 1845, was the last person to live there. It was during 1974, however, that the end of a long era finally arrived when, at 89, the last of the traditional rope-makers, Mr Bert Marrison, finally retired. A few years later his ashes were interred just inside the entrance.

Watching a demonstration of rope-making by our guide, we were intrigued by the ingenuity involved with tops, runners, sledges and the spinning of the hemp twine itself, the operation being completed with the Marrison Loop – characteristic of all rope produced in the Peak Cavern during recent times. Rope was very important to the lead-mining industry in many ways, from tethering pack-horses to winding packs. Moving on, our guide drew our attention to the large stalactites, formed over thousands of years, hanging from the ceiling of the show cave. Some had assumed all sorts of shapes that set the imagination awry.

Along the narrow path that led down to the Bell House, we met the cave air proper, which remains at a constant temperature of 9 degrees C, making it feel fairly warm in winter and cool in summer; this chamber, so we were told, being part of the complex drainage system. Following heavy rain storms, the water table rises profoundly throughout. Where we stood, the waters could actually rise to the height of the roof, and flow round the back of the ropewalks and out through the main entrance. As they recede, a mixture of water and air would be sucked down through a tight fissure, producing a loud farting noise, the reason for the cavern being nicknamed the 'Devil's Arse', to the disdain of Victorian society.

An exceptional phenomenon like the Peak Cavern would once have been regarded as a creation of the Devil. This was when strict religious beliefs were regarded more highly than knowledge and common sense, thus the place became more and more steeped in folklore and superstition. Small wonder that many of those earlier visitors would have arrived with a combined feeling of dread and fearful curiosity. The deeper down they went, so the nearer to Hell they would have believed themselves to have been.

With backs bent, our group of investigators next passed through 'Lumbago Walk', emerging by a small pond, the Inner Styx, where two varieties of freshwater shrimps thrive happily. In one respect, being so far underground (with over 400 ft of limestone above our heads, going back millions of years) I felt that we were no bigger than those freshwater shrimps by comparison. In another, having also been 'in touch' with those more recent rope-makers, made me feel that we were Time Lords, licensed to pass from one age to another.

I noticed the ferns and lichen that grew in small quantities on the damp, rocky surfaces, as a result of the lights being switched on throughout 'business hours', the tiny spores having initially been brought in on tourists' clothing. Recalling the visit that Dilys and I had made to the famous Aillwyce Bear Caves in Ireland, I remembered that the lights there switched on automatically as visitors passed through in stages. As they moved on, so the lights behind them switched off, to discourage any such vegetation becoming established.

Our exciting tour through the Peak Cavern continued, as we were reminded that for two or three hundred years, this incredible place would have been part of the Grand Tour of Derbyshire – a must for all well-off travellers, in spite of the lead-mining in the area. While our ordinary footwear was perfectly adequate on the day, visitors in earlier times both men and women, would have found themselves – wearing their smartest clothes, of course – almost up to their waists in mud. Hardly the best calling-card for visiting the next place on their itinerary, Chatsworth House!

We were suddenly reminded of our true mortality on seeing what looked like a coffin lined with straw. This was the craft in which earlier visitors were required to lie down while a guide, up to his waist in water, pushed with one hand, while holding a lighted candle in the other, under an extremely low arch, then the only way into the Great Cave ahead. When the young Princess Victoria paid her first visit to the Peak Cavern in 1834, so we were told, she too had to lie flat in the craft. From a different source, however, I learned that she actually refused to go near the craft, at the same time declining to go any further into the Cavern. On her second visit as Queen in 1842, a tunnel had been blasted so that she was able to walk through; this being the only man-made feature of the whole cave system.

We too walked through the tunnel to the Great Cave, 150 ft in width, 90 ft long and 60 ft high, according to the guide book. Quite remarkable on realising such places had been formed by the dissolving and scouring action of water, reaching high up into the roof, especially from the age when the ice sheets were melting at the end of the last Ice Age. One could imagine the awesome power unleashed at the time.

Another passage led us to Roger Rain's House, where water cascaded dramatically *ad infinitum* from Lady Well, a short distance from the ruins of Peveril Castle above, built by the Normans. The drops were finely illumined silver and gold when we were there, and with water dripping from the roof in certain places (though nothing fierce), wearing a hat was definitely advisable. High up on the rock wall of this inner cave we were surprised to see a balcony vividly lit. This was where a local choir would have entertained the gilded visitor, and if he was displeased at their performance, his guide would explode a measure of gunpowder which 'rolled along the roof and sides like a tremendous and continued peal of thunder'. This chamber is known as Pluto's Dining Room. The only source of light in past times would have been candles, and our guide offered to switch off the lighting briefly so that our group could sample the experience of being entirely in the dark. Consent was unanimous, though one lady said that she was afraid of the dark – but would keep her eyes shut!

It would be tempting to say that to Helen, Dilys and myself, the darkness seemed all-embracing, comforting, with a sense of protection issuing from the massive field of energy of the surrounding rocks, an energy field that would have dwarfed even those of the biggest forest trees. But of course, that was our perception through our knowledge in the 21st century. We would have reacted far differently if like early man, we had been alone, clad only in animal skins and facing what would have seemed like eternal darkness; here rational thought would have been suspended in a completely different dimension. Even more recent visitors might have perceived things just as awesomely with only candle-power to light their way; the rope-makers, who were familiar with the caves in which they lived in comparative squalor, certainly jumped at the opportunity to act as guides to the rich traveller who would have gladly 'crossed their palms with silver' to be shown through such a hostile environment.

The rope-makers themselves, being local people who in those times probably never travelled out of their locality, were more likely to be referred to by 'more worldly' people who came to experience the place, as 'cave dwellers, troglodytes, and beggars who stank and lived in little hovels'. In 1683, however, a Mr Hobbes, suitably impressed by his guide, wrote:

'...a she Native of the place,
Handsome enough and girl enough she was,
Who with her steady foot and accent clear
As guide emboldens us with many a cheer.'

As far back as the 13th century, it was recorded that various chambers had been magnets for many 'rogues, knaves and vagabonds' – places of safety that the normal, law-abiding citizens of Castleton would have avoided. The most notorious 'no-gooder' was Cock Laurel, last 'King of the Beggars' who organised the get-together for the Beggars' Banquet held annually in the Peak Cavern, during the latter part of the13[th] century. The beggars had permission from the Crown to hold their feast during two weeks in the year and fearful of nothing or no-one, it was said that on one occasion Cock Laurel even invited the Prince of Darkness himself.

Nowadays, the organisers stage various attractions within the Peak Cavern – choral concerts, Proms in the Peak and recreations of the Beggars' Banquet are featured as well as ghost walks by candlelight. Our guide told us that (not surprisingly) a psychic had indicated that there were many spirits still around in this dark place. Speaking for ourselves though, both Dilys (as a psychic) and I thought that the atmosphere of the Cavern, in general, reflected the age of the great rock formation and this seemed to predominate, as though any 'hauntings' by man had never been allowed to establish themselves; that the great age of the environment had simply dismissed them, in spite of any questionable deeds committed in the past.

Away for the moment from the material world, the hushed reverence and sense of wonder experienced when we first entered had adapted to the sound and/or sight of running water but (in the same way as being among forest trees) there was still a sense of mystery to me – a sense of being watched. But by whom or what? In such a place the atmosphere seemed far deeper with mystery than in the presence of possible ghosts. There was a sense of the presence of some God – or Goddess – the mythological deities of old.

I felt we were experiencing an intimate connection with Mother Earth herself as well as the natural life implicit in the rocks. They, together with the water, made up such an incredible environment in unknown quantities netted by time, that though God-created, man still tries to add something – to leave some sort of imprint no matter how. On a nearby rock face in Pluto's Dining Room, many bygone visitors have carved or scratched their names in order to record their visit – these include Lord Byron and Charles Cotton, the 17th century translator and poet.

We had now penetrated deep into the complex of caves and standing by a waist-high barrier at the far end of the same cavern, faced a set of mysterious, descending steps. We could hear the roar of rushing water in the Devil's Cellar far below, the so-called River Styx (named after the Greek Goddess of the Underworld) which, mythology tells us, flows through Hell. In real terms, this was the same source of water that had flowed out (though more calmly) from under the cliff as we entered the Cavern at the start of our visit.

I could not help feeling that the Peak Cavern, like similar places, is actually a blend of its own massive field of energy with that of everyone who has worked, lived or visited over such a long period. We all leave behind us something of ourselves – our imprint – wherever we go. Hence, a new public venue just opened, like a theatre, concert hall or sports stadium, can feel dead and dry to begin with, but ten years on that same venue will have accumulated a completely different atmosphere – of warmth, life, excitement, as well as a sense of history and a firm relationship with the future.

As we stood listening to the tumult of waters far below, our guide pointed out the presence of a narrow concrete gulley to the left side of the steps; this, he explained, was the work of the BBC when they filmed an episode of *Dr Who*, in which the Doctor slid fearlessly down into the dark abyss; his visit more than appropriate, since it added another well-known name to the list of visitors who had paid their respects to the Peak Cavern. And comparing his imprint with those of our own, he remains undoubtedly one of the most genuine Time Lords of all!

SUPERNATURAL SNIPPETS No 1
Doom & Disaster

1 – The Maniac Driver

Down the ages many people – including those who never thought themselves particularly psychic – have occasionally experienced fractional glimpses of past happenings. These need not necessarily have been of great events, more likely replays of everyday routines folk might once have undertaken. The brief glimpse of a monk, for example, busily digging along what might appear to be a solid path, on the site of what was once a monastic herb garden; or someone seated on a weathered stone bench; a young person bursting with joy over some good news from years back; someone older in the depths of despair. However brief, the happiness of the former and apparent negativity of the latter might well have been sensed also. Even the smell of cigarette smoke is often a sign that spirits are around, as is the scent of lavender or perfume. Indeed, such brief encounters are best regarded with wondrous curiosity as opposed to fear.

But there are instances where caution might be the best approach. Dilys and I had a strange experience when returning home from Sheffield by car one evening in early March. We were passing through Millers Dale in Derbyshire along the narrow B6049 – a particularly strange, very atmospheric road, even by day, for this is where motorists have occasionally reported being pursued by a fierce phantom dog. Whether it has any connection with the fact that during the 16th century, the last wolf in England was shot in the nearby village of Wormold, is anyone's guess.

We were making our way up through the surrounding rocks and trees towards the main A6 Buxton to Bakewell road with no other vehicles in sight, when from out of complete darkness, headlamps – on full beam – were suddenly switched on, two or three feet behind us. In the rear view mirror, I saw what appeared to be a white Ford Transit van right on our tail. It was alarming, and I was tempted to pull up and ask the driver what he was playing at, especially as the vehicle seemed determined to 'hug' the rear of the car as we continued our way up through the trees. Whenever I slowed down, the van simultaneously did the same; and because of the frequent bends in the road, I knew he couldn't overtake. On pressing the accelerator, we both increased our speed – again uncannily at the same time.

'Keep going, don't stop,' Dilys urged, uncharacteristically panicked by our strange encounter.

In the strong reflected light the driver looked in his early thirties, stocky, with closely cropped hair or shaved head. With dogged determination he was still in pursuit, staring hard at us. Then I realised, again through the rear view mirror, that he was not staring at us but *through* us! We careered as fast as I could safely drive along the final bends in the road and into sight of the main A6 – seconds later, the lights from the van switched off as suddenly as they had first come on. There was now complete darkness to the rear and checking through the mirror again I could see the white van had vanished. We knew the driver couldn't have pulled off anywhere at that point. We had passed the only place – a natural lay-by under overhanging rock – where he could have parked, a quarter of a mile back.

So did we encounter a ghostly van and its driver? Was he a spirit who did not realise he was dead? (For that matter, did we know he was *really* dead?) It was difficult to say, bearing in mind the different dimensions we appeared to have been in. Had we, however briefly, been intruders in his reality experiencing some sort of time-slip? Perhaps that was why he wanted us out of the way – or did he not see us? I wondered afterwards if this phantom vehicle might have 'passed through' our car if I had performed an emergency stop, but I was not prepared to take the risk!

Dilys and I had used that road before and have done many times since, by day and night without further incident. On that occasion, maybe we stumbled by chance on the anniversary of some tragedy that had happened along that stretch of the B6049 in the fairly recent past – taking into account the phantom was a white Ford Transit van. Was it a paranormal replay of the incident? Who knows?

2 – Crashed!

The complete disappearance in 2014 of a Malaysian air-liner with nearly 240 people on board, made us wonder how this was possible, despite highly sophisticated tracker-systems world-wide in constant operation. Some people might even claim it was abducted by aliens into another dimension. But whether any wreckage is ultimately found, we may never know what actually happened on board during those final hours of Flight MH370 before it plunged into the sea, or into some other mysterious fate.

Although circumstances may have been somewhat different, the occurrence brings to mind the earlier case of New York to Miami-bound Eastern Airlines Flight 401. Approaching Miami Airport, as they attended to a warning light regarding faulty landing equipment, both Captain Bob Loft and his co-pilot Don Repo failed to realise the excessive speed they were travelling at as they descended. The plane crashed into the Florida Everglades on the night of 29th December, 1972; of the 176 people on board, 101 were killed on impact, Bob Loft dying shortly afterwards, while Don Repo survived only till the next day.

Because the Everglades consist mostly of water, some parts of the plane were found to be undamaged. Thus Eastern Airlines decided to recycle them as 'spare parts' for other Tristar l-1011 airliners in their fleet.

It was then that strange things began to happen and ghostly sightings of Bob Loft and Don Repo were reported by various air crews, shortly after some of the planes had been fitted with the 'spare parts'. The three-dimensional figures of the dead captain and his co-pilot were sometimes seen in the actual cockpit and galley on different Eastern Airline flights. In one instance, a flight engineer about to carry out his pre-flight check on board one plane, came to the flight deck and saw someone sitting in his seat at the control panel. It was recognisably Don Repo, the late co-pilot of Flight 401, who told him that there was no need to worry, because he himself had already done the pre-flight check. Then he instantly disappeared.

The spirits of Loft and Repo seemed mostly concerned about points of safety when flying a plane – landing equipment problems that might be encountered, for example, or possible fire hazards. It was as though they were both deeply concerned that the fault that had downed Flight 401 should, at all costs, be avoided by every Eastern Airlines flight crew in future.

Further paranormal events included a vital tool suddenly appearing in the hands of a flight engineer, a sudden surge in the jet engines of one plane while flying, which avoided catastrophe, and phantom voices speaking about safety through the public address system on board a sister aircraft.

Eastern Airlines, though somewhat sceptical regarding such claims, did offer to fund counselling sessions to all those crew members involved – and they also replaced the salvaged Flight 401 parts on planes in their fleet that might have received them. Once that had been done, the ghosts of Bob Loft and Don Repo were never encountered again.

Eastern Airlines no longer exist. Yet why did the ghostly sightings of Loft and Repo happen in the first place? Arguably, it was the weight of responsibility and guilt on their consciences, for the original verdict on the cause of the accident had blamed not just equipment failure but human error. The tragedy of Flight 401 was thoroughly researched and written up by writer John G. Fuller – renowned for his studies about UFOs – the book becoming a best-seller in 1976, and ultimately, a gripping movie on TV.

3 – In the Depths of the Forest

For many of us, our native woodlands have always been places of secrecy and sensory awareness. Our distant ancestors not only viewed them as hunting-grounds and a source of fuel, but also as havens of strange, undefined presences. Even today we may pick up, as our forefathers did, the same feeling of being closely surveyed. In woodlands entities seem to still exist in a dimension where past and present overlap and become connected.

At Dinnington, near Rotherham, West Yorkshire in 1862, an ancient barrow was excavated in which twenty skeletons of men, women and children were found. Having elongated skulls, they were thought to be Neolithic, about 40,000 years old. Although the barrow was situated in woodland, houses were built close by during the 1960s and ever since, both residents and visitors have frequently witnessed ghostly figures clad in light-coloured clothing watching them intently – not only from close to the barrow, but also from among trees nearby. The watchers then disappear, leaving a very cold, spooky atmosphere in their wake.

Possibly from more recent times, a stampede of ghostly horses has been encountered by a number of individuals in Down Wood, Blandford, in Dorset; they have been forced to quickly jump out of the way for fear of being trampled under the numerous hooves making their thunderous approach. Expecting to see the distressed animals pass by at any moment, the individual has been left completely puzzled when nothing more occurs than sudden

47

silence. Investigations have shown a complete absence of trampled vegetation or broken twigs, let alone any trace of hoof-marks in the soft ground. The origins of this strange, unseen 'replay' cannot, as yet, be traced.

Paranormal 'sound effects' have also been picked up on the edge of Salcey, an ancient and once royal forest several miles south of Northampton. It was here in July 1830 that a bare-fist fight took place between Alex McKay (the 'Highland Hercules') and a local man, Simon Byrne. After slugging it out through 47 rounds, McKay was to die of his injuries the following day; his opponent, charged with murder, was ultimately granted an acquittal. Because of the high emotional involvement during this extreme 'sporting event', it is said that blow after blow can still be heard resonating through the trees, together with grunts, groans and bouts of laboured breathing. Some visitors even claim to have seen both blood-soaked pugilists, stripped to the waist, in desperate combat, the vision quickly fading until only the sounds remain, including faint cheering from phantom supporters.

In the village of Pengrugla in Cornwall stands a haunted, ancient oak tree, a former hanging tree which is the perfect setting for intrigue and mystery, especially with an overgrown patch of un-consecrated ground behind the 500 year-old oak; here the bodies would have been interred. Strangely, no official records were kept, suggesting that hangings occurred on an irregular basis, possibly as a warning to the local populace; though equally as strange is the fact that no excavations have been carried out to confirm whether or not such interments took place.

From the site of an excavated Roman fortress against a wood near Aylesford in Kent, there emerges the figure of a Roman centurion still apparently carrying out his watch. Might his spirit have been disturbed during the excavations? And are those hanged souls allegedly interred among the tree-roots at Pengrugla resting peacefully? According to some, the atmosphere already seems well-populated with unseen presences. Even today, many people still believe that trees (like flights of steps and stairways) act as powerful conduits between our own world and the higher Spirit World, which could make the possibilities endless.

4 – Pools of Mystery

Mysterious pools in out-of-the-way places have always been the stuff of legend. Some are reputed to be bottomless, while others supposedly contain treasure. Near to the River Tees, on the outskirts of Darlington, are four mysterious deep pools known as Hell's Kettles. According to local gossip: 'Spirits have oft been heard to cry out of them'. On one occasion a farmer obstinately ventured out on St Barnabas' Day (June 11th) a public holiday when everyone else officially had the day off. Passing the four Hell's Kettles with his hay cart, he was just one more victim to be drawn down into their strangely troubled waters. Fate had decreed that his horses, cart and all should suffer the same perilous demise – and his ghostly team has been sighted there a number of times since.

On Bodmin Moor in Cornwall, not far above Jamaica Inn (made famous by Daphne du Maurier) is situated the wide, sombre Dozmary Pool, believed to be bottomless. It is steeped in Arthurian legend; here dwelt the Lady of the Lake who first gave to Arthur the sword Excalibur. Later, according to Alfred, Lord Tennyson, the dying Arthur commanded Sir Bedivere to throw it back into the lake – and an arm clad in glittering white samite rose from the water to catch it, waving it three times before vanishing into the depths.

Such mysterious pools can sometimes have a strange custodian in the form of a mermaid! In the Derbyshire-Staffordshire Moorlands area, on Morridge Moor, there is such an isolated pool known as Blake or Blackmere. Here the mermaid has the dire reputation of suddenly appearing, snatching her hapless victims from the bank and dragging them into the deep and acidic waters to drown. A spectral arm has also been seen reaching up from the middle of the pool on a particular date in the year, and several murders have supposedly been committed in the vicinity. No wonder local people refuse to walk past the isolated spot after dark.

At Mill Hill near Chapel-en-le-Frith, there is a pool where tradition has it that on Easter Eve at midnight, if you look hard into the waters you are certain to see the mermaid. And many sinister tales still surround another Mermaid's Pool, a large expanse of marsh water below Kinder Downfall, high above the Derbyshire village of Hayfield. Although said to be avoided by animals and birds, the local people regard this as a place of magic. Here, a beautiful nymph who lived in a cave in the side of Kinder Scout would emerge each day to bathe in the waters. Anyone fortunate enough to see her bathing was awarded the gift of immortality - unless the nymph happened to be in a bad mood, in which case the witness was unceremoniously dragged down to a watery demise.

Mermaids are supposed to have been seen in many parts of the country. In Suffolk, the River Gipping was believed to contain a number of them, although most tended to have lived in local pits and pools. At Child's Ercall in Shropshire, two workmen passing the local pool, some centuries ago were told by a mermaid that treasure lay at the bottom and they were welcome to have as much as they wanted, provided they jumped into the water and took it from her hands. They waded in up to their chins and the mermaid reappeared, taunting them with a piece of gold the size of a man's head. Then, laughing, she disappeared – with the gold. Whether the workmen drowned or managed to scramble out, wet but wiser, was not made clear.

Rostherne Mere is reputed to be the largest and deepest of its kind in Cheshire. On Easter Day, a mermaid may be heard singing as she rings a sunken bell. During a peal at the local church once, it is said that the heaviest bell broke away and fell at the water's edge. Successfully recovered three times it fell yet again, a workman finally cursing it as it splashed into the mere. Another version concerns the bells of Combermere Abbey which now hang in Wrenbury Church. At the time they were being ferried across the mere, one of the bells fell overboard. The man in charge cursed it - and within a few seconds, a huge monster heaved itself up from below, dragging him and the bell down, never to be seen again. The monster was believed to have been Jenny Greenteeth, who once haunted stagnant pools of green slime and ate children, though as far as the mermaid was concerned, she could have entered the mere by way of a subterranean channel connected to the Irish Sea via the River Mersey. The smelt, a saltwater fish that breeds in fresh water, once inhabited the mere, so the idea of a subterranean access to the sea may actually be close to the truth.

As mermaids of the sea drowned sailors, so inland mermaids lurked in rivers and isolated ponds waiting to drown passing travellers, especially children. Belief in mermaid-type forms reaches far back to times when the Celtic goddesses, along with other deities, were widely worshipped across various swathes of the country, a belief which seems to have persisted in part, well into the first half of the 19th century. Such mermaid pools might also have been used for ritual human and animal sacrifice.

5 – The Terror of Tunnels

Whether serving road, rail or water, tunnels have always been a source of mystery and danger, whether still in regular use, left neglected, or even bricked up. Each of these domains of darkness has its own story – usually supernatural – wherever it may be located in the world. The Yokosuka Naval Base in Japan boasts many tunnels, including Gridley Tunnel where, between midnight and 1 am, the lone motorist may suddenly come face-to-face with a terrifying spectral samurai. Believed at some time to have been killed whilst carrying out instructions from his lord and master, his spirit, honour-bound, seems still intent on completing his task – whatever that might be.

By the completion of the Hoosac railway tunnel in North Adams, Massachusetts in 1851, it was already being referred to as 'The Bloody Pit'. Five miles long, having been cut through the side of a mountain, over 200 men died during its construction. There had also been an explosion, killing a further two men instantly. Kelly Ringo, the man who had inadvertently caused the accident, was unharmed but on returning to work afterwards, was later found dead, having been strangled. No-one was ever accused of his death, but locals believed that the angry spirits of the two construction workers had returned to exact their revenge. Ever since, ghostly lights have been seen along the tunnel, and echoing cries of agony from those who perished during the building of the tunnel have frequently been heard.

Closed to rail-traffic in 1919, the Redbank Range Tunnel in Picton, Australia (which had also been cut through a mountain) was put to a number of uses over the years, including that of a mushroom-growing farm. One day back in 1916, however, forgetting to check the train time-table, Emily Bollard, a local girl, decided to use the tunnel as a short-cut to visit her brother's farm on the other side of the mountain. Hearing an approaching train, she desperately tried to escape but in vain; her mutilated body was caught up on the cow-catcher and transported to Picton.

Soon afterwards Emily's ghost was seen nearby, as well as in the tunnel. The spectre of the train that struck her, too, was spotted. Witnesses along the tunnel also experienced a drop in temperature and strong movement of air as the phantom train passed through at speed. These days, the tunnel is closed – except for access to organised ghost walks!

One of the longest tunnels in Britain, Wast Hills, carries through it the Worcester-Birmingham canal. This is where the spectre of an old working narrow-boat has been seen, before evaporating into the brickwork. Alarmingly, a number of people once reported a woman standing in the bow of their pleasure-boat, pointing to the far end of the tunnel, possibly as a warning that another craft was approaching. As she turned, they saw a look of absolute horror on her face before she disappeared.

Next to the award-winning Black Country Living Museum is the much-haunted Dudley Tunnel, some of whose spirits go back to the days of the Industrial Revolution. Yet many crews who manoeuvre their pleasure-boats through the tunnel actually pick up a feeling of sheer happiness! They have even been aware of a gentle voice making comments like 'Well done!' and 'That was easy, wasn't it?' Sudden (but not scary) laughter can also be heard ringing out in some of the larger caverns.

Meanwhile, outside on the canal bank sits *Diamond*, a tired old craft awaiting much-needed restoration. This is regularly visited by a ghostly old boatman – possibly a former owner – who sits in the stern in order to check her condition and keep her company. Obviously, he takes heed of folklore suggesting that boats – particularly if constructed in wood – possess souls of their own that need constant nurturing.

6 – Echoes of Battle

Areas of highly traumatic action in the past can still vibrate with echoes of the clash and firing of arms. No matter from what period of history, these would have been scenes of intense, emotional activity, extremes of bravery and determination, where every individual would have been fighting for his very survival.

Such energies, perhaps held in the fabric of buildings, terrain or even in the atmosphere, appear to be released or 'played back' during times when conditions are right and are thus termed as being 'cyclic'. They can take the form of the actual appearance of possible phantom soldiers, the 'smell' of battle, or even horrific sound effects alone.

Huge battles can still occupy places where acts of violence on a large scale occurred in an atmosphere of physical mutilation and death. Young men dying years before their time in large numbers, programmed to cling on to their human condition until the last possible moment, could well have been responsible for creating a build-up of traumatic energy, thus 'recording' their plight in a particular location.

The monument known as Neville's Cross at Durham, for instance, gave its name to a battle fought in the vicinity during October 1346 between the Scottish Army under King David II, and that of Queen Philippa, the wife of the English King Edward III, who was away fighting in France at the time. During August of that year he had achieved a great victory at Crecy over the French King Philip VI, who in desperation had requested his ally King David to attack the English in order to divert the attention of their army.

In response, the Scottish king, having set alight Lanercost Abbey and ransacked Hexham Priory, was only two miles from Durham when the Archbishop of York, together with the Bishops of Durham and Lincoln, with Lord Neville of Raby and Lord Henry Percy, hastily assembled a host of 16,000 men to defend St. Cuthbert's shrine (and their own estates). Surprisingly, they managed not only to defeat the Scots but also to capture their king.

According to local tradition, the sounds of ferocious fighting could be heard emanating from the site for many years afterwards. In Victorian times, a boy who often visited the site claimed that the sounds of battle, including the clash of armour, could be clearly heard if you put an ear to the surrounding turf, having first walked nine times round the monument.

Similarly, May 22nd 1455, saw the Battle of St. Albans, Hertfordshire, the first conflict of the War of the Roses between the reigning Lancastrian family and the Yorkists, headed by Richard, Duke of York. It is said that on the anniversary, ancient properties since built on the supposed site of the battle resound with the determined clash of opposing armies.

I discovered while pursuing my research for *Ghosts at War* that battle trauma seems – with the possible exception of romance – to be responsible for most spectral activity. Though my book covers a huge time-span from what is possibly the earliest recorded ghost (a primitive man on horseback) to the end of World War Two, I am still coming across incidents new to me, as well as uncovering unexpected connections with other forms of ghostly activity.

I found that large phantom Black Dogs, with blazing eyes the size of saucers, can haunt old roads and are especially active in places of high tension and trauma. Old routes come under their scrutiny, especially those taken by armies and the phantom hounds are said to be connected with the passing of Bonnie Prince Charlie and his Scottish Army in December, 1745. Their dark shadows lurk particularly near the graves of many Jacobite soldiers killed in the retreat, ghost soldiers who defiantly haunt the Old Route right back up to the Scottish border and beyond.

7 – Cars with a Jinx

In the mid-1950s the actor James Dean had achieved an iconic status with which American teenagers strongly identified, especially in his role as the angst-ridden teenager Jim Starky in *Rebel Without A Cause*, his most famous film. According to Marjorie Garber, he had 'the indefinable extra that makes a star'. But behind his celebrity and less well-known, are the strange facts that surrounded the high-performance car in which he died when only in his mid-twenties.

Iconic film-star Dean's other ambition was to be a racing driver and at intervals between making movies like *East of Eden* and *Rebel Without A Cause,* he took part in a number of racing events in Palm Springs, Bakersfield and Santa Barbara. But Warner Brothers banned him from racing during the making of what would be his last film, *Giant.*

The film completed, and accompanied by a support-team, he left Hollywood at high speed in September 1955 heading east for a weekend's sports car-racing at Salinas – Dean at the wheel of his recently-acquired Porsche 550 Spyder. Meanwhile, in late afternoon, along Route 466, another car was travelling at speed going east. As it crossed over the centre line to turn onto Route 41, heading north, Dean, who was travelling at an estimated 85 mph, had no time to steer clear of the other car. The vehicles crashed almost head-on. On impact, the Spyder – the lighter of the two vehicles – shot into the air and spun before landing on its wheels in a ditch nearby. Dean, suffering from a broken neck and several other serious injuries, was pronounced dead on arrival at Paso Robles War Memorial Hospital some 28 miles away. At the inquest, the verdict was to fault his reckless driving; the other driver, Donald Turnupseed, a university student, being cleared of any blame.

James Dean was laid to rest on October 8th, 1955 at Park Cemetery in Fairmount, Indiana. But his doomed car seemed to take on a life of its own. When the wrecked Porsche was taken to a garage it was reported that the engine fell out, breaking both legs of a motor-mechanic; later, a doctor who purchased the engine to replace the one in his own competitive car, was killed when racing shortly afterwards. Another fatality in the same race was that of a driver of a car fitted with the driving-shaft from Dean's Porsche. Subsequently, a fire broke out at the garage where – probably because of his celebrity status – it had been decided to rebuild the Porsche. At Sacramento, where the car went on display, it broke a teenager's hip when it fell from its mount. At a later date, the truck which was carrying the celebrity car smashed into a shop front on its way through Oregon. Finally, in 1959, supposedly secure, it inexplicably collapsed into several pieces while supported on stationary steel supports.

There is a fascinating comparison with a similar case from more than forty years before. This followed the assassination of the Archduke Franz Ferdinand and his pregnant wife Sophie during a state visit they paid to Sarajevo, in Bosnia on the 28th June, 1914. This was one of the events to trigger the terrible First World War. Their luxurious Graf & Stift limousine was sold on many times afterwards, each successive owner (an unlucky thirteen in all) being injured or killed as a result of various accidents involving the jinxed vehicle – nowadays safely confined within the War History Museum in Vienna.

There are many people who would say that coincidences are merely random events, totally disconnected to each other. But none other than the psychologist and philosopher Carl Jung often cited the pioneering work in Extrasensory Perception carried out by American Professor J.B. Rhine, as 'objective evidence of an active force behind coincidence.'

The case remains open.

8 – Devil's Advocate

Some years ago in a much-publicised report, psychologist Dr Richard Wiseman claimed that ghosts did not exist. He and his team from the universities of Hertford and Edinburgh came to this conclusion having investigated two of the most haunted places in Britain – Hampton Court and Edinburgh's South Bridge Vaults. Both sites have been connected with 'inexplicable temperature changes and a sense of a presence,' he stated. A large number of people were asked to visit these places, as part of his inquiry. Unsurprisingly, the outcome was that locations where things had felt unusual corresponded with areas previously thought of as being haunted. Dr Wiseman, and his team, however, believed that it was more 'normal' things that contributed to what people believed were paranormal happenings.

He suggested there were variations in local magnetic fields, room sizes and levels of lighting. Those who felt they had genuinely experienced strange phenomena had, he believed, merely experienced 'certain environmental stimuli that people are not consciously aware of.' Wiseman also added that 'these findings strongly suggest that hauntings do not represent ghostly activity, but rather of people responding unwittingly to normal factors in their surroundings.'

His findings were published in the *British Journal of Psychology*. Though to include comments like 'we believe' and 'are probably due to' in this type of report hardly smacks of sound, scientific evidence in my view. And the evidence that ghosts exist is far stronger, despite the fact that they are entities that exist in another dimension.

Lines of natural energy – ley lines – in the ground (meaning Dr Wiseman's 'variations in local magnetic fields' perhaps?), particularly where they converge, can attract supernatural activity to a particular location – especially where underground waters or caverns may be found, as we saw earlier. But to go blundering 'cold' into any place in an attempt to encounter a ghost will for the most part, prove to be futile – as is well-known, they are not performing animals and we are far more likely to 'wander into' their dimension unintentionally.

People who are psychic are certainly able to encounter ghosts. Or at least, sense a presence by means of sound, or smell – pleasant or otherwise – or even intuitively. Those who are not psychically attuned will experience nothing – though in fact, most of us are psychic to a greater or lesser degree, as I have stated a number of times in my books.

People who argue that ghosts do not exist, I think, are missing out on the wonders of an extraordinary dimension, a huge and boundless reality in spite of the existence of ghosts not being 'scientifically' proven. They are afraid not of 'spooks' as such – but of the fact that the paranormal is something inexplicable and beyond their control. Ghosts have been encountered by people since the beginnings of civilisation. Mankind has always been aware of the existence of a world far beyond the temporal - '*A vital breath of more ethereal air,*' as Longfellow put it.

The thinking person will continue to support the enquiring human mind. But do we really need to know the answer to every single mystery? Including those relevant to the various gods, or spirits of our ancestors which, in some parts of the world, have in themselves attained deity? Perhaps Dr Wiseman should take note that if there had been any suggestion of mass deception regarding things paranormal, it would surely have been revealed as such long before now.

PART TWO
THE MYSTERIOUS UNIVERSE

4 SURROUNDED BY AIR

Of the four elements, air is the only one we cannot see, represented by sky, wind and storm. Importantly it is also a shallow layer covering our planet, being what we breathe, in addition a source of good feeling, inspiration and atmosphere. Many ancient cultures believed that the Earth was the territory of the goddess, while the sky was ruled by the gods. Being able to see through air, we are not only nurtured by the sun but take in the appearance of our fellow beings, animals, and the everyday objects we depend on, domestic or otherwise – like Wordsworth and his rainbow too, the wonders of Nature.

Looking through a window, our impression may be restricted by the confines of the window itself. But standing outside, we are faced by an entirely different prospect. A panoramic stage offered by the great outdoors – and even beyond – enables us to glimpse the lapwing's spectacular courtship display on wing each spring, the V-shaped formation of migrating geese high in the autumn sky. We can appreciate places as diverse as the Fenlands of East Anglia – John Constable country with its huge, ever-mobile skies – to the seductive might of the snow-capped Himalayas, the physical (and to some, the spiritual) roof of the world.

Air has its power, too. There are times when landscape can be dramatically blotted out – sometimes with serious consequences which can take their place in the mysteries of the unexplained. In November 1948 a US B-29 Superfortress, part of a photographic Reconnaissance Squadron, was on its way from RAF Skampton, Lincolnshire, to Warrington in Cheshire. The craft got lost in thick low cloud, crashed and exploded 1,600 feet up on the summit of Bleaklow near Glossop, in the Peak District, killing all thirteen of the crew, including the captain, Landon P. Tanner.

In 1997 several visitors to the area saw what they thought was an aircraft flying erratically, eventually crashing high up on Bleaklow. Rescue workers were quickly summoned but nothing was found, apart from partially buried, abandoned pieces of the original plane. What the eye-witnesses had seen was a phantom re-enactment of the Superfortress's final moments on that fatal November day back in 1948.

Prior to the disaster, the aircraft (nicknamed *Over Exposed)* had been involved in reconnaissance work over the Russian Zone during the Berlin Airlift of 1948. Formerly attached to 509th Composite Group (atomic bomb unit), Pacific, it was part of a reconnaissance team whose mission it was to photograph the atomic bomb tests on Bikini Atoll in the summer of 1946.

Some years later, a man searching through the debris on Bleaklow found a wedding-ring. As he was showing it to a friend who was with him, both men became aware of the phantom figure of Captain Landon P. Tanner standing nearby, watching them intently. The two men hastily retreated, although the finder of the ring later did some research and sent it to Tanner's relatives in the United States.

Further investigation was made involving the use of an ouija board. Contact with members of the crew indicated that, spiritually, they were unable to rest in peace and felt doomed to roam the area for ever, a memorial near Bleaklow Head commemorating them as victims of the tragedy. The Peak District, an area where a number of plane crashes occurred during and shortly after World War Two, remains an eerie place, particularly when shrouded in mist.

When I interviewed Tony Smith, a retired civil servant, he told me about the time when he and a friend interested in aircraft went to the crash site on Bleaklow. Viewing the scene, they distinctly heard what they could only describe as a burst of disembodied barrack-room laughter as they were walking past what remained of the 'Super's' fuselage.

A more famous area of strange, unresolved repute is that of the Bermuda Triangle, situated between three geographical points - from Miami in Florida, to Puerto Rico in the Caribbean, to Bermuda. Besides the mysterious disappearance of ships, some without issuing a single distress signal, the fate of a number of planes has also been unaccounted for.

Towards the end of 1945, five American TBM Avenger Bombers took off from Florida, heading eastwards over the sea on a training exercise; their flight path of 300 miles was scheduled to bring them back to base. In spite of excellent weather conditions, however, they never returned. The pilot in charge had at first radioed that all was well. But two hours later, contact with all five bombers had been completely lost. A search plane with a crew of thirteen was scrambled - that, too, disappeared without trace.

For many decades it has been believed that such mysterious occurrences are caused by supernatural elements. One theory concerning the Bermuda Triangle is that the area, also known as Devil's Triangle or the Hooda sea, is haunted by the troubled spirits of millions of slaves who for reasons of death, illness or even as punishment, were thrown overboard from ships taking them from West Africa across to the West Indies and the southern United States, during the days of the slave trade.

Whether this is true or not, exorcists have tried to free these troubled spirits, which seem to be sufficiently numerous to take possession and confuse the minds of air pilots and ships' captains, with fatal consequences.

Two years before the disappearance of the TBM Avenger Bombers, Dr Kenneth McCall, an exorcist and medical surgeon, was returning home from a lecture-tour of the United States. He and his wife, along with the crew, became stranded aboard a banana boat in the eastern section of the Triangle when the ship's engines failed. For five days they waited for help to arrive; the vessel drifted but the weather was good and there was a positive atmosphere on board. During this time Dr McCall and his wife clearly heard sounds of rhythmic chanting. Since there was no other explanation for them, they assumed these were being made by members of the crew, but when help finally arrived and Dr McCall mentioned the chanting to the crew, they denied any such thing. The doctor was perturbed enough to record that he believed the sounds must have come from the spirits of those unfortunates sacrificed to the waves and sharks over the gruesome years of the slave trade.

There are people who believe the Bermuda Triangle to be some sort of electrical field inexplicable to logical reasoning, which can navigate earthly objects and beings into some other dimension, pictured high up in the heavens. (The old gods trying to make a comeback, perhaps?)

As well as recognising space as representing the indefinable distance between the heavens and Earth, we often talk of needing our own 'personal space' in which to live. According to Paul Auster, the American novelist and film director, 'Life is wandering around in space and bumping into objects.' The ground may shift under our feet, yet the conscious mind is able to find stability in the weightlessness and vastness of space – a private space nonetheless, in which, incorporating his earthly experience both positive and negative, the creative artist (among others) is able to absorb ideas or even divine inspiration. As Elgar once put it: 'There is music in the air' – the notes of which he was able to capture by writing them down. There are also musical instruments heavily dependent on air in order to be heard, by having to be blown – flute and piccolo, clarinet, trumpet, tuba, horn, trombone, alpine horn and others. Regarded as particularly spiritual is the wind-chime, moving gently in the air breeze, producing relaxing sounds that are able to lift our thoughts to a higher level.

Judy Garland used to sing *'Somewhere Over the Rainbow'*, encouraging us via Hollywood 'glitz' to 'wish upon a star'. If this sounds romanticised and over-glamorous it is nonetheless based on the truth that man's vision has always been focused on finding out what was 'up there'; his aspiration has been to fly with the birds, reach for the moon and other planets in our solar system, to lose himself among the stars.

Since the start of civilisation, man has regarded the skies with both fascination and trepidation – this is the realm of the old gods who moved about freely, unrestricted by gravity. According to classical mythology, Iris was their swift-footed messenger who trailed her beautiful scarf, the rainbow, across the heavens. Icarus, an earthbound mortal, equipped himself with wings of wax in an attempt to reach that seemingly forbidden territory. But flying too near to the sun, his wings melted and he came crashing down to Earth.

Punishment for such audaciousness seems always to have been harsh, although not necessarily reserved solely for mortals. Lesser known was Phaeton, the son of Helios (the Sun), who one day drove his father's chariot (the 'Car of Fire') recklessly across the heavens on its journey from east to west. Unable to control the highly-strung horses, he plunged from the heavens, his body ablaze as it fell into the River Eridanus, far below. After Phaeton's remains were buried his sisters, who had supported his ambition, were transformed into black poplar trees on the riverbank, their tears turning to amber as they mingled with the fast-flowing waters.

Within our human history the artist Leonardo de Vinci, who lived in the 15th century, was the first to draw his idea of a flying-machine – but it was to be half a millennium before man's knowledge of scientific engineering, physics and design enabled him to evolve machines that were heavier than air, yet capable of being flown. By the First World War (1914-18) the air had become an inevitable theatre of conflict which, potentially, it still is to the present day. Many of us have seen the iconic 1941 newsreel footage of people in a rural environment, as they stared anxiously at the zig-zag vapour trails in the sky during the Battle of Britain. Now the news every day features modern pictures of war in the air in all parts of the world, which we can view by personal screens so small we can carry them in our pockets.

Advances in technology saw broadcasting begin in the early 1920s, where sound waves were, as if by magic, transmitted through the air at the start of this age of 'modernism' and mass communication. Has this signified the end of the old gods – their *Gotterdammerung*? We might wonder if God and man have abandoned each other, especially during the course of the 20th century, in the face of what science has apparently had to offer as an alternative.

In October 2012, a worldwide YouTube audience of 8 million sat on the edge of their seats as a forty-three year-old Austrian, Felix Brumgartner, plunged into the stratosphere wearing a space-suit from a capsule fixed to a balloon nearly 25 miles above the Earth. Almost immediately there was concern in the command centre as he went into an uncontrollable spin, but regaining control and having descended into a denser atmosphere, he managed to open his parachute and nine minutes later landed safely near Roswell in the New Mexico desert. Breaking the record for the fastest freefall through the sound barrier (690 mph) he briefly touched 833.9 mph in the less dense stratosphere.

Yet here was a man who, despite the technology that had got him there, felt himself confronted by one of the essential truths of our existence. Of the moments before his epic jump, Brumgartner said: 'When standing on top of the world, you become so humble, you do not think about breaking records any more, you do not think about gaining scientific data. The only thing you want is to come back alive.'

Despite our record-breaking age – including getting to the moon and sending up equipment to research distant planets; its sophisticated aircraft and missiles capable of carrying weapons of mass destruction – fleets of commercial air-liners and smaller business aircraft, alternative fleets of smaller 'flying machines' continue to exist for purposes of more leisurely pursuits. The individual person can fulfil his sense of adventure by way of hang-gliders, hot-air balloons, private planes, traditional gliders, micro-lite aircraft – and more recently by drones.

The element of air has been the setting for many reported supernatural happenings.

In January 2005 flight attendants on board a Korean Airline plane noticed that a seat had been vacated by a woman passenger in her mid-thirties. Investigating the bathroom area, they found that she had tragically hanged herself with her scarf, and attempts to revive her failed.

Over the following months strange incidents occurred on board the same plane – unworldly voices were heard plaguing the crew, cold spots were felt in certain places – and it was thought these indicated the presence of spirits drawing energy from the air, possibly also from the living people who were present. During one flight a Buddhist monk, the sole first-class passenger, began to carry out ritual chanting: when asked if anything was wrong, he remarked that the empty seats around him were all occupied by dead people. An off-duty crew member became aware of someone tucking him in with his blanket as he took a nap and, opening his eyes, saw a phantom hand protruding from the side of the cabin. The crew obtained holy water in order to bless the bathroom area in an attempt to free the plane of its unwanted 'passengers' – but all to no avail. Following numerous complaints, the Airline eventually withdrew the plane from service.

Three years later, during a flight by the same Korean Airline, another passenger committed suicide in the same way – by hanging herself with a scarf in the bathroom area. Was this a grim coincidence, or had the Airline secretly reinstated the original plane?

Except for a short pleasure flight as a teenager during an open-day at RAF Shawbury in Shropshire, I had no experience of air travel until a few years ago. Boarding a BA plane early one October morning, Dilys and I left behind a rain-soaked Manchester Airport, on course for Shannon in Southern Ireland; this short stay was to include our visit to the Aillwyce Bear Caves, which I mentioned earlier. I found the combination of rain and endless cloud casting gloom across the heavens very much seeming to absorb us. The plane rocked slightly, like a boat, reminded me that there was nothing below the floor except for a 14,000 feet drop between us and the ground – or the sea - below. I gripped the seat tightly, reassuring myself that everything would be fine.

Miraculously, the rain surrendered to a rising sun and the memorable spectacle of bank after bank of huge cumulus clouds of dazzling white backed against a sky of mellow autumnal blue, reflected in the placid sea below. No longer gripping the seat, I had a sensation similar to the one I was to experience on my later visit to the Peak Cavern - that this was another world in which we passengers and the plane felt so minute. Little wonder, I thought, that man has always believed that wisdom in the form of God, or the gods, originated from the skies (as well as in the case of the cavern, from the element of deep earth). Later, gazing on the land mass below with its numerous small fields, each bounded by its precise hedging, I had my first glimpse of Southern Ireland.

Prior to our return to the United Kingdom, a savage gale had been blowing for two or three days of our short break. It still continued as our plane took off in the evening from Shannon Airport. Climbing, we were rocked, dipped and dipped again as the Atlantic blast took us. To my relief things settled as we headed slightly north-east; the turbulence pushed us at a fair speed from behind and all was well until the pilot had to manoeuvre the plane in order to land in Manchester. We turned straight into the gale. The plane was bucking and pitching violently, my stomach felt as though it was colliding with the inside of my skull. Then (seemingly miraculously) we were safely down, very glad to be back on *terra firma*, amid the warmth and reassurance of our own familiar world.

5 NEW GODS FROM SPACE

'It was coming straight for us, we thought it was going to hit the car. We ducked below the dashboard, terrified, thinking we'd had it!'

These words were no hyped-up dialogue from some weird sci-fi film but a very factual report told to me of an incredible 'close encounter' with an unidentified flying object (UFO) experienced by a middle-aged couple from Staffordshire. There are many people who have had encounters with UFOs, of course and mankind has always felt it has been watched by 'something' in space – whether perceived as various deities, even the sun and moon, meteorites, shooting stars and (for a want of better description) those ubiquitous UFOs. These are unfamiliar and unaccountable crafts which, according to witnesses over the years, are seen in various shapes – saucers, cigar-shapes, triangles or whatever. Often brightly-lit, they are also capable of incredible acceleration and deceleration of speed, defying the laws of physics. Wherever they originate from, it has also been claimed that individuals have actually been abducted by the aliens who man them, sometimes taken aboard such craft and returned to earth later.

Why should no-nonsense people, having encountered a UFO, be accused of being attention-seekers just for the sake of it? Everyone I have interviewed concerning their experience of a UFO, or any other paranormal activity, has come over as truthful and sincere. One can tell simply by common sense and instinct. In some instances, they may have been slightly hesitant to begin with, trying to gauge my reaction. But realising they were talking to someone keenly interested they have tended to 'open up' – sometimes for the first time, or at least in so much detail, since their experience.

In 1950, Daniel Fry, a missile engineer, claimed that a UFO landed near to him while working in New Mexico. Hearing voices asking him to step aboard, he did so. Next thing he knew he was being taken on a round trip over New York and back in under one hour! During the journey a voice told him that expeditions from the UFO's home planet had been coming to Earth throughout history to try and help Mankind, but had not yet met anyone of 'sufficient intelligence'. Adding to the mystery, Fry later accused the American CIA of suppressing his story for many years. In 1978 near Plymouth, a woman claimed that while hanging out her washing in the garden she was grabbed by three aliens – each about 5 ft in height, in metallic blue suits – and beamed into a craft hovering overhead. 'Aboard, there were these other aliens, sort of,' she said. 'But I never felt threatened.' The next thing she remembered was being back in the garden. Looking up, somewhat stunned, she saw the spacecraft rise into the sky at great speed and disappear.

More sinisterly, there are those people who report that following abduction they had not been able to remember anything. Only after the event were they able to recall under hypnosis what really happened. Some have said to have been physically examined, even operated on. Following such encounters of this 'intimate kind', their health has sometimes deteriorated – apparent diagnosis of such cases having shown radiation sickness.

I was particularly excited at the prospect of interviewing Ted and Rita Armstrong and getting a genuine insight into their strange experience. Over coffee in their comfortable home in the North Staffordshire Moorlands area, they told me a truly amazing story. Basically, the facts were that they were driving home from a visit to Longnor (a small village on the high moors) late one Saturday night in March, 1999. Conditions, according to Ted, were 'very clear, with no wind at all. The road is high up and you can see right over Leek (the market town where they lived) to the lights of the Potteries, about 15 miles south.'

Ted and Rita pinpointed their position as some way from 'The Winking Man' pub, which is at the junction to the main Leek to Buxton Road; they were heading towards the pub when they saw an incredibly bright light in the sky, roughly a mile to the south. Oblong-shaped, it seemed to be 'trembling', according to Rita.

Ted added: 'It moved slightly towards us as we continued along the road for another two or three hundred yards. Rita was driving and, more out of curiosity than anything else, I told her to stop the car.'

As she did so, the alien craft, with ever-increasing brightness, headed straight for them at an incredible speed, the light filling their car. They ducked beneath the dashboard, expecting a terrible impact. Nothing happened, and after a period of some seconds they warily raised their heads.

'We looked up. The craft had stopped outside our car,' Rita continued. 'It was still facing us, slightly to the left, about 40 feet away, hovering some 50 feet above the ground. It was still very, very bright, a kind of light we had never seen before. The closest description Ted could find was that it was like a welding light. The strange thing was that even though it was incredibly bright, there was no shadow cast whatsoever. All the light was contained within the craft and our car and the grass and moorland around us was in the dark. From underneath the craft there seemed to be a white, smoky haze billowing upwards. Then suddenly two wings or ramps opened out from the top, reaching down to the ground.

'Then I saw somebody – or something,' Rita went on. 'A very tiny figure low down on the right-hand ramp in the rising haze. It looked like a kind of fairy wearing a short silvery skirt, consisting of what seemed like a lot of folds and fabric. It had long, bright yellow hair flowing down its back. The face was blurred, but with two arms it was steadying itself, or hovering in the haze. I didn't know which.'

Ted, a builder by profession, described the craft as narrow in width, about the size and height of a terraced house, though he saw no figure, only the bright light. 'But there was no doubt in our minds that the thing definitely knew what it was doing. It came directly at us and I have to say, we were scared out of our wits.'

I asked Ted and Rita if either had felt any sense of communication with the visitor(s) who might have been in the craft.

'I did, I had a great urge to get out of the car and see what this 'thing' wanted,' Rita admitted. 'But the whole episode happened so very quickly and Ted was shouting: 'Let's get out of here'.' As the car pulled off the grass verge, they saw the UFO rapidly raise its ramps.

'It seemed to power up, with white clouds coming from underneath as it took off,' Ted recalled. 'We didn't feel any heat and there was no noise either as it shot off at great speed towards Leek, then headed away over the Potteries very high in the sky, all within a few seconds. It went at a tremendous speed!

'We both felt a lot better when we'd seen it go, but I still wanted to get onto the main Buxton Road – then home, quick as possible! As we drove on – several miles more – neither of us said a word, I suppose we were in shock, in trauma. It was only after we'd closed the front door that we were we able to describe what we'd actually seen, like a 'letting go' of tension.' Ted admitted honestly that 'if I had been on my own, I might have concluded I'd dozed off for a couple of seconds while driving and dreamt the whole episode. But the thing was - we both saw it.'

I was particularly interested that Ted and Rita made no reference to any malfunctioning of their car engine whilst so close to the UFO and its potentially powerful magnetic field. In similar cases (although not all) it has been reported that an internal combustion engine may lose power, or even stop altogether in such a situation. If switched on, headlamps too have been known to dim or go out. Conversely, according to witnesses, as an increase in distance occurs as the UFO moves away, the car engine or lights will resume function as normal.

Although his car was not affected enough to be brought to a standstill, Alan Cave, a businessman from Taunton, Somerset was driving along the Stroud to Gloucester Road one morning in October 1982 when his vehicle passed beneath 'an orange cloud type of craft', as he later described it, hovering in the sky. Over the car radio the announcer said it was 11 am, but Cave noticed that his watch suddenly read 10 am and his digital pen indicated 9 am! Both had been correct only a few minutes earlier. He also noticed that his car was 'losing' hundreds of miles because the speedometer was rapidly going backwards! Fortunately for him he was able to keep driving, which may well have saved his sanity, even his life.

Mysterious encounters with aliens, their space-craft and even trips aboard them to far-off galaxies have been reported as a result of allowing the power – whatever it might be – inherent in meeting up with a UFO to take control. And bearing in mind that Rita admitted experiencing the urge to get out of the car having seen the 'fairy' that night in the North Staffordshire Moorlands she was probably very lucky she did not do so. As Ted commented, he would have been regarded with the upmost suspicion had he told the police his wife had been abducted by a UFO! Grim humour, this, but if Rita had somehow disappeared, it would have been no joke.

I wondered about the threat or fascination of possible abduction when I spoke to another couple, John and Linda Harvey. Their UFO encounter had happened some 17 years before in

Worksworth, Derbyshire when they were driving with their children Carl (10) and Karen (8) on their way to celebrate the twenty-first birthday of Linda's brother. 'About three-quarters of the way up Wash Green,' they reported, they spotted a distinct triangle of lights in the sky.

'We were very puzzled, so we stopped and watched this thing,' John recalled. 'It was probably bigger than a plane, hovering about 50 ft up for a good two or three minutes, I'd say.'

There was no sense of communication, and they did not think it was going to land. 'It was just that we all went very cold - including Carl and Karen,' Linda said. 'You know that shuddery feeling, as though someone was walking over our graves.'

'And then it just suddenly vanished,' John added, 'so fast none of us knew in what direction it had gone.'

Although perhaps less gripping than the encounter Ted and Rita had experienced, to John and Linda and their children this was an event that made such an impact they will always remember it. In my own experience of interviewing people who have had UFO sightings – and Dilys reports the same in similar cases she has dealt with – those concerned usually insist: 'I know it happened. I know I didn't dream it. I saw what I saw, and I will never forget it'.

Dilys recalls an occasion when she was a teenager. 'My boyfriend and I were out shopping like everyone else, it was on a typical Saturday afternoon in Wrexham (in North Wales, the town where she lived), spring-time, I think, a sunny day with no clouds. I just happened to glance up and saw two objects high up in the sky, above the shop buildings on either side of the street. They looked like silver balls, the sort you put on cakes for decoration – although they could have just been reflecting the sunlight. It was impossible to determine their size, because there was nothing to refer to. And there didn't seem to be any signs of doors or windows, just round silver balls.'

Asked for her initial reaction, Dilys said: 'Just interest, really. I discussed with my boyfriend what they might be. We didn't experience any strange feelings or electrical sensations, like some people have reported. We watched them for some time. Then one suddenly shot off to the right, very fast; there was no sense of acceleration and it had gone within a second or two. I've never seen anything move so fast as that, after simply 'hanging' in the sky as opposed to hovering. Then the other started to move in the opposite direction, but very slowly. We tried to follow it but couldn't because it went out of sight behind the rooftops.'

Dilys shrugged. 'We did try to report what we'd seen to the police, but they weren't interested, even though I'd drawn diagrams. We even got in touch with the nearest aerodrome, same thing. We told our relatives, discussed it with friends – but we knew nobody who was any authority on the subject, no-one really knew how to handle a potentially supernatural occurrence - and perhaps I should add here that most people behave the same way now.'

Most incidents of a supernatural kind are likely to happen purely by chance. And more often than not, people feel unable to talk of their 'unearthly encounter' to anyone – not even to relatives – for fear of being ridiculed, or suspected of mentally 'cracking up'.

The Romans observed that particular Celtic sky gods and rituals involved the constellations at certain times, involving the Pleiades group of stars in particular. Animals and birds, too, by way of their natural behaviour at different stages of the year were regarded for their special part in divination, while the Druids themselves were said to have achieved magical flight, though more of a transcendental than physical kind.

During the so-called 'Cold War' (1950s and 1960s) when there was a spate of UFO sightings, questions were anxiously asked of the reluctant authorities. Were flying saucers actually real; or were they sophisticated weapons being developed by America or by the former Soviet Union? People became increasingly puzzled, especially when authorities on all sides refused to comment. Or even to admit UFOs existed at all.

UFOs first came into popular prominence when the term 'flying saucer' was first coined by Kenneth Arnold, an experienced pilot, in June 1947 after he caught sight of nine of them flying in formation close to the Cascade Mountain tops in Washington State. But although the label 'flying saucer' may be a recent appendage, the phenomenon obviously is not; in fact, UFOs in various guises have been reported throughout history – and they do seem attracted to certain locations on Earth. Places in America, Brazil, parts of Europe have all reported sightings. In the UK, Salisbury Plain, Broadhaven, Wales and the Peak District, for example have been particularly notable, and reported sightings world-wide appear to have increased over the last century.

Apparent UFOs are recorded in the Old Testament, such as in the Book of Ezekiel, where frightening objects and their means of transport are presented as mythic and angelic. UFOs were even regarded as 'demon ships' in Ireland in 1000 AD; and it was in Lyons, in France, that possible 'space travellers' were killed in 840 AD. The monks of St Albans, Hertfordshire, saw a UFO in 1284. Shortly afterwards, in 1290 the Abbot and his monks at Byland Abbey, Yorkshire, told how 'a large, round silver disc' flew over them at tremendous speed. Numerous other sightings were witnessed, such as giant, glowing discs covering the sky over Basle in Switzerland, in August 1566, causing the population to panic. Sightings too were reported twice over London in 1741 and in 1748; also over Ebrun, France, in 1820. Over the next seventy years more were to occur in America.

There is even a theory that beings have been brought by UFOs to live on Earth from a planet that is no longer habitable, also that some super-race – with individuals ranging in height from 4ft with large heads, to 7ft tall giants in silver suits – seems sympathetically concerned about the possibility of mankind actually destroying itself. So perhaps they are 'holding off' a mass landing for fear of causing panic or a breakdown of 'earthling' society. (Some people believe this was to have occurred as the Second Coming in 2000 AD).

Majority opinion holds that UFOs and their crews pay us visits from Outer Space. But Ted Thoben, an investigator from Connecticut, has suggested that certain locations here on Earth may actually be portals – magnetic deviations in the landscape – where UFOs can pass through. So do they actually occupy the same space that we do, but in a different dimension? Thoben also suggests that less obviously, the portals may be a part of our everyday experience. Is this what gives our countryside a curious feeling of wonder and fascinating mystery, more prevalent in some areas than others? Perhaps our hunter-gatherer ancestors sensed this more keenly than ourselves, especially where life or death was concerned. Small wonder they took to reading the weather, season, air and atmosphere – all the rituals of what they believed were the ways of the old gods.

6 WHEEL OF FIRE

From ancient days Man has been in awe of the mysterious and powerful element of fire. Our own early encounters with fire probably included learning how to strike a match, enjoying hollowed-out turnip or pumpkin lanterns with their ghoulish faces lit by candles to celebrate Hallowe'en, or joining in the excitement of a community bonfire with its glittering display of fireworks on 5th November. We might have watched a skilful blacksmith in the heat of his mobile forge, demonstrate the making and fitting of horseshoes at an agricultural show. But such activities hint only at the huge potential of fire itself, one of the most spectacular elements known to man; its kinder side provides us with warmth and light, as well as helping us to carry out many commercial processes – as well as cooking our food.

The true means of heat in our solar system is the sun; and Mabon 'the Sun of Light' is the solar god particularly associated with the Druids. In its physical form fire can bring people together for warmth, it not only keeps wild animals at bay but converts matter into energy. Man has always felt he was in direct communication with the gods by means of rising smoke as well as by flame – when smoking his pipe, the native North American Indian felt he was in touch with the spirits. Fire is the great cleanser and purifier. Yet out of control it becomes a vicious destroyer, a wildfire or an erupting volcano possessing the terrifying power to annihilate indiscriminately, good as well as bad.

In Ancient Egypt the great Re', depicted as a man with a falcon's head on which he wore a solar disc, was regarded as the supreme generator of life and chief sun-god, widely worshipped in Heliopolis, in Lower Egypt.

Many myths described Re' and his daily journey across the sky. Rising at dawn in the east to clamber aboard his 'day-boat' with a few ardent followers, he travelled throughout the day, and arrived in the west by evening. Then aboard his 'night-boat', he coasted along for the next twelve hours providing light for the 'other world' (the other side of the earth) before starting his 'day' journey all over again. Hostile powers and cosmic beings incessantly challenged the sun-god in his bid to maintain order, but with help of the cobra Uraeus, 'the pride and sharp eye of Re', such alien interference was quickly seen off.

To the Ancient Greeks the sun was Helios, fire having divine qualities throughout the sanctuaries of the land, including those at Olympia. The Olympic Flame, symbol of the Olympic Games originated here, where it was kept burning for the duration of the ancient Olympics at the altar sanctuary of the goddess Hera. Celebrated too, was the fact that fire was stolen by Prometheus from the Greek god Zeus to give to man, so additional fires were lit at the temple of Zeus himself (to whom the ancient games were dedicated) as well as being maintained at the altar sanctuary of Hera, his wife. Today the Olympic flame is lit at the place where her altar once stood, by means of direct sunlight concentrated by a parabolic mirror – the element of fire being reintroduced at the Amsterdam Summer Olympics of 1928, and upheld ever since. In contrast to the original Olympic flame in Ancient Greece, however, the current practice of transporting the lighted torch all the way from Greece to the various designated Olympic venues throughout the world is a modern one, introduced at the 1936 Summer Olympic Games in Berlin.

Adapting to the changing seasons, early man first cultivated grain crops on realising the power of the sun – the greatest ball of fire he knew – which he, too, came to regard as a deity as it passed daily across the sky. Two 15th century engravings show the divine pair of Brother Sun (Sol) and Luna, Sister Moon, both having reached the Autumn Equinox and gathering darkness late in the harvest season. Symbolically this was when Sol returned to the

Underworld, either as the 'dying' Sun or as the sacrificed Corn King which, with renewed vigour, would hopefully return to provide a good harvest the following year. The engraving reveals that between Sol's feet sits Leo, the Lion star-sign which he governs. On the other engraving Sister Moon, depicted at the same turning-point of the season, stands astride of Cancer the Crab, the watery star-sign which she rules.

Worshippers offering prayers would light bonfires in the belief that this would increase the strength of their sun-god, especially during the pagan Celtic Samhain (1st November), in order to add power to the waning sun and to ensure its return in the spring. Later this custom was modified (being held on 5th November) to celebrate the Gunpowder Plot and its failure to destroy King James I and Parliament in 1605. Samhain was to become All Saints' Day and for Pagans and Christians alike, November became associated with the cult of the dead when for a short while, the veil between the 'quick and the dead' was lifted.

Supposedly, the spectacular burning of a Viking-style ship each January in the Shetland Isles has certain echoes of the Celtic Festival of Samhain. Known as Up-Helly-Aa, this is also carried out to encourage the return of the sun at winter's passing, although this apparently ancient ceremony has its origins in comparatively recent times. It is thought possible that early worshippers made a first attempt at Stonehenge (built around 4,000 years ago) to actually chart the solar system. Despite the fact that the true purpose of the site is not known, modern sun-worshippers (including members of the Most Ancient Order of Druids) gather there each year on 21st June to hold an all-night vigil paying ritual homage to the midsummer sun.

Situated in the Staffordshire Moorlands, the market town of Leek where Dilys and I once lived, still experiences its mystical Double Sunset on Midsummer Eve. Having set behind a hill called Bosley Cloud, the sun reappears to its right before setting again in the normal way. Once a major spectacle that attracted crowds of people, today it has become less apparent due to a possible tilt of the Earth's axis.

A source of great heat and light, the sun-god was also regarded as a pursuer of order, not just of the four seasons but also the important periods of time within those seasons, indicating when best to sow crops and when to harvest them (with slight year-to-year fluctuations according to the weather). Interestingly, with the sun appearing to move clockwise across the sky, the ancient sun-worshippers made sure their ritual processions and dances were also performed in a 'sun-wise' direction.

At some fire festivals in Europe, burning barrels of tar swung around poles and the practise of throwing fiery discs into the air were supposed to evoke the magic, or mimic the sun. The burning of the straw man and other effigies was regarded as sacrificing the Earth-King, whose ashes were scattered on the land to ensure a bumper harvest for the coming season.

Sir James Frazer tells in his classic book *The Golden Bough* how some early peoples reacted to an eclipse of the sun by firing blazing arrows into the air, hoping to rekindle the ebbing light; while members of the Sensis tribe of Peru also aimed burning arrows at the sun during an eclipse, not particularly to reignite the sun but to see off some savage mythical beast deeply-seated in their culture, which they believed was threatening its life-giving energy.

And nearer to home, as recently as 1851 in Lancashire, it was reported that: 'If any householder's fire does not burn through the night of New Year's Eve, it betokes bad luck during the ensuing year; and if any party allow another a live coal, or even a lighted candle, on such an occasion, the bad luck is extended to the other party for commiserating with the former his misfortunes.'

The Birth of Christ, the Light of the World, saw several pagan festivals eventually absorbed into the Christian tradition. For example, the Yule Norse Renewal Festival with its burning logs and candles, symbolising the rebirth of the Sun God (though not a Celtic fire-festival as such) became part of Christmas, representing the Light of Life.

Hitherto, the blazing Yule log, a block of olive or beech-wood – though more usually of oak – was said to indicate the number of calves, kids, foals and chickens that would be born in the coming year, by the number of sparks it produced when struck. If a piece of log was put on the land it was believed to act as a fertiliser and give protection against hail. Another old belief was that if the remains of a Yule log (especially of oak) were kept indoors for twelve months, they gave protection to the dwelling-house, particularly against fire and lightning. This may have derived from the Nordic belief that the oak-tree had magical connections with Thor, the god of thunder.

Even the symbolic lighting of brandy poured over the Christmas pudding, which we are all familiar with, has its roots going back to the pagan worship of fire; also the northern European custom of the candle-lit coniferous Christmas tree. This was believed to shelter the woodland spirits during the winter, when the deciduous trees were without their leaves. A Christmas tree was reputedly first seen in the streets of London during the 15th century, although Prince Albert is credited with having introduced the custom into our homes in the early 1840s.

Candlemas Day (2nd February) was regarded as the Feast of the Purification of the Virgin Mary, when mothers who had borne children during the previous year attended church, bearing lighted candles. As a ceremony of flame, this went back as far as the 5th century, originally part of the Roman Festival of Februa, when candles were carried through the streets and the purification rites of the women were respected. With the establishment of

Christianity, the important May Day festival became superimposed on the pagan Beltane celebrations. This was when the Celts would have celebrated the start of summer by honouring the sun, lighting great bonfires.

Among the many superstitions connected with Easter, one widespread belief concerning Easter Sunday was that when the sun rose on that particular morning, it appeared to dance! In 1895 it was reported: 'On Easter Sunday, the people of Castleton, Derbyshire, used to climb the hill on which the castle is built, at 6 o'clock in the morning, to see the sun rise. On the Wednesday before Easter Sunday a Derbyshire man, full of excitement, was quoted as saying: "I think the sun will hardly be able to contain himself till Sunday."'

The martyrdom of St Clement on the 23rd November was another important date on the Christian calendar. This was when the Saint was said to have been lashed to an anchor and drowned; he was later adopted as patron of ironworkers, his feast day being celebrated until recent times. Gathering at Twyford, near Winchester, the ironworkers would ceremoniously perform 'firing the anvil', in which gunpowder was rammed into a small hole in an anvil before being ignited. A procession followed, at the head of which an effigy of St Clement was carried round the village, with money being collected for a feast at the local hostelry, The Bugle Inn.

Considering the important role of ironworkers in primitive society, there are many legends regarding the Saxon smith and wizard, Wayland; it was he who forged coats of mail, amongst other things, for the pagan gods in a much older festival of smiths that could well have preceded the celebrations for St Clement on that day. Roughly a mile west along the Ridgeway from the White Horse of Uffington, on the Berkshire Downs, is situated an empty burial chamber at least 5,000 years old, known as Wayland's Smithy even long before the Norman Conquest. Legend tells us that after the coming of Christianity, Wayland, usurped from his position as smith to the Norse Gods, was forced to shoe horses for mere mortals for a living. To this day, it is said that if anyone leaves their horse, and an old sixpenny piece on the capstone by his chamber, on their return the horse will have been shod and the sixpence gone.

Amid the fire and sweat of the forge, where Wayland crafted swords and weapons of war, other objects of beauty, crafted in precious metals might also have once possessed their own connection with war. In Wagner's opera *Das Rheingold*, the dwarf Alberich stole the Rheingold from which he forged a magic ring (the ring of the Nibelung), a ring that became involved in the power struggle of love and corruption.

7 THE STAFFORDSHIRE HOARD

Together with Dilys and our friend Helen, I visited a collection of ancient treasures of the goldsmith's art, the unique Staffordshire Hoard Exhibition at the Potteries Museum and Art Gallery in Hanley, Stoke-on-Trent, when the Hoard was first put on display to the public. Visitors found themselves confronted by a stellar display of incredible craftsmanship in miniature, tiny, priceless objects which were the products of a warring society.

The Hoard was discovered in a muddy field near to Lichfield, by means of a metal detector in 2009. It consisted of 1,662 individual pieces in gold and silver, representing at least five kilos of gold and half a kilo of silver; there were also hundreds of pieces worked in garnet – all thought to have been buried there since 600 AD. Unlike the well-known Sutton Hoo find, excavated near Woodbridge, Suffolk in 1939 just prior to World War Two, expert opinion doubted if the Staffordshire hoard was in any way connected to a burial. Staffordshire was at the heart of Anglo-Saxon Mercia, probably the largest kingdom in Britain at the time. With expansionist ambitions, however, it was particularly aggressive during the 7th and 8th centuries and the Hoard may have represented the spoils of war assembled by Mercian kings Penda, Wulfere or Athelred during their campaigns against East Anglia and Northumbria.

Here was a savage age, ruled by savage leaders who were inspired by tales of noble pagan heroes such as Beowulf. Doubtless, much blood would have been spilt as paganism struggled against the coming of Christianity. Mercia was one of the last Anglo-Saxon areas to convert in the mid-7th century, albeit slowly; and in fact, at least three crosses are included in the find. Perhaps Christian hordes even attacked fellow Christians – the victors stripping the arms of the vanquished of all valuable embellishments – even golden crosses being wilfully damaged. Considered a highlight among the finds was a strip of gold thought to have come from a cross, bearing a war-like inscription from the Vulgate version of the Bible, which in translation, reads: *'Rise up, O Lord, and may thy enemies be dispersed and those who hate thee be driven from thy face.'*

It is almost certain that much of the hoard was collected following conflict, perhaps even from the dead who still lay on the field. Most of the embellishments, made of precious metals, were seemingly ripped from swords or armour and crushed up together. With the noted absence of swords themselves, it seemed that the objects in the Staffordshire Hoard were carefully selected and not just scrap gold and silver. At the time of looting, the metal swords, from which a lot of the precious fittings had been torn, were probably reused by the victors or recycled as new weapons.

It is possible that these were votive offerings made to propitiate the gods, as was the practise of the Ancient Celts. Many weapons of war have been found in rivers, lakes and springs. Offerings of cauldrons, weapons and even chariots (2nd century BC to 1st century AD) have been discovered by archaeologists, particularly in Welsh lakes such as Llyn Cerrig Bach on Anglesey and Llyn Fawr in Glamorgan. A possible god of war may have been associated with the River Thames, whose waters have yielded helmets, swords and shields in the recent past. A spear-head with gold inlay, also discovered, may have been made purely as a votive offering rather than a weapon of war.

The artistry inherent in the items of the Staffordshire Hoard is incredible, particularly since many of the pieces are so tiny they have to be viewed through a magnifying glass to fully appreciate the skill of the goldsmiths, jewellers and engravers. Notably, the gold hilt of a single-edged sword, intricately decorated with animals and set with exquisitely-cut garnets, is adorned with two facing birds, presumably eagles, which may have been attached to the straps that held the sword in its scabbard.

Many pieces are engraved with animals – some easily identifiable, others unknown mythological beasts. Anglo-Saxons highly respected the horse, and a number of horses were discovered engraved on a helmet finial, the helmet fit for wearing by a high-ranking warrior or even a king.

In a general collection of small items there are several small snakes made of gold, some with pins on their undersides, which Dilys believes could have been votives, precious offerings to a god, or gods, or even pieces worn and taken into battle as lucky talismans for protection. The Druids believed that the snake (or Nathair, the adder) with its sinuous ability to crawl into the dark inroads between the rocks, connect it to the Underworld and the Realm of Death. Able to shed its skin, as the totem animal of the Earth Goddess and the Sun God, it is said to represent our own ability to die and to be born once more, which might have appealed to Anglo-Saxon belief.

We also saw garnet-inlaid gold strips, possibly scabbard mounts, book-cover mounts or saddle fittings. Particularly striking was a glass gem with a similar gold and garnet setting, possibly from the Celtic west; also a small gold buckle, plain except for a band of filigree around the rivets.

The job of cleaning the Hoard of its Staffordshire soil was a painstaking and ongoing process, we learned. A technique had been developed using thorns, strong enough to rid an object of soil but flexible enough not to damage even the most delicate gold filigree. We marvelled at the incredible skill of the craftsmen of those times. Either they had exceptional eyesight or some means of magnification at their disposal, which we now know nothing about. These were the Dark Ages – meaning that the Anglo-Saxons from Mercia were not literate, thus leaving no written records – but many questions surround the discovery of the priceless Hoard. Some of the exhibits are so unfamiliar we do not know exactly what they are, or the function they once fulfilled. According to one of several helpful leaflets issued by the Museum: 'some objects resemble finds from other sites, but many pieces are unique and there is nothing to compare them with.'

We found ourselves speculating along with the experts as to the secrets of this amazing collection. Had the Hoard been hidden by some individual who died before he could retrieve it? Was more than one person involved? - (considering the size of the find, this seems more than likely). Did the Hoard represent the spoils collected by numerous scavengers after one battle, or many? It has been suggested that the entire Hoard may have represented 'booty' seized by Penda, the last pagan Anglo-Saxon king, who ruled his territory of Mercia from 633-655 AD with great ruthlessness following his campaign against Northumbria. Yet, had it finally been buried hurriedly at the threat of possible invasion by another enemy? Techniques in detection are helping to find the answers to some of these questions – for instance, it is believed the gold originated from quantities of Byzantine and Roman coins being melted down while the garnets, surprisingly, are thought to have come all the way from the Indian subcontinent by way of trade routes established even then.

To the Anglo-Saxons, the figure of the eagle was a sign of sovereignty and possibly associated with the worship of Thor and Woden. Among other incredible finds in the Staffordshire Hoard was a curled swastika, skilfully created with four eagles' heads in gold, which might have adorned a shield. The symbolism of the swastika reaches back into history, despite its implications during the 1930s and '40s. The four elements of earth, air, fire and water represent the four arms of what is known as the 'cross of matter', a vital symbol in Celtic art, included in the Sun Wheel. This four-fold division is believed to have been worked out originally by the

Greek philosopher Aristotle (382-322 BC) and for the Celts it became a focus of worship as they tried to harness the elements through sympathetic magic. The pagan Anglo-Saxons would also have connected the symbol with Thor, but more particularly with the great God of Fire – the very Sun itself.

The period of the Staffordshire Hoard was one of great change; over 650 years Anglo-Saxon England gradually evolved from being a tribal society. By the death of Alfred the Great in 899 AD it had become a single, unified country, with a template laid down for the English language. And even today we may still participate in ancient rituals without realising it. Only a few weeks ago, Dilys and I were standing in the Rows in Chester watching a street entertainer – a fire-eater!

SUPERNATURAL SNIPPETS No 2
The Mysterious Universe

9 - Rain, Rain

'The rain is falling all around,
It falls on field and tree,
It falls on umbrellas here,
And on the ships at sea.'

This poem, included in Robert Louis Stevenson's *A Child's Garden of Verses*, says it all. Often confined to his sickbed as a child, it would be easy to imagine the author looking out of the window, watching as a wet world goes by.

Despite the fact that water so brilliantly sustains our lives, even today the prospect of a rainy Monday morning hardly inspires confidence at the start of a working week. So the rhyme 'Rain, rain, go away, /Come again another day', readily comes to mind, one of several learned in early childhood. These form a direct link to earlier generations of children who recited those very same words, from as far back as the 17th century, as a charm which was believed to influence the weather. The whole subject, 'Whether the weather be fine/ Or whether the weather be not' – especially with regard to rain – is steeped in folklore.

Many well known sayings to do with the different seasons have originated in the same way, based on shrewd observation of natural events, particularly by the old country dwellers close to the land. This was, of course, long before it was possible to 'tune in' to the weather prospects for the day courtesy of the all-present media now on offer at the start of the 21st century. For example there was an old adage: 'Black frost, long frost /White frost, three days and then rain.'; another decreed: 'Long foretold, long past/Short notice, soon past.' (This refers to the fact that a storm may brew for many hours before it breaks, whereas a short sharp shower can fall from a mere passing cloud). Two more sayings: 'The farther the sight, the nearer the rain' – and 'Sound travelling far and wide, a stormy day will betide' speak for themselves.

Some beliefs have almost been forgotten, while others are still of easy recall, despite their origins having faded into the mists of time. As we know, a wet July 15th supposedly prophesises forty days of rain. But Saint Swithin, who disliked pomp and circumstance, is said to have brought this retribution on his followers when his remains were transferred from a common graveyard for reburial within Winchester Cathedral. Similarly October 28th (St Simon and St Jude's Day) had a reputation akin to St Swithin's Day – with good reason, for towards the end of October, the fine weather will normally begin to break and the winter gales begin. An occasional variation from the usual run of things enabled a few late tasks on the land to be completed in relative comfort.

In many parts of the ancient world, civilisations looked with awe to nature and consulted their gods for information about the weather. According to the Aztecs it was their rain god Thaloc, a sky serpent, who was responsible for creating massive storms by ejecting rain from his enormous stomach which contained all the waters of the heavens. Meanwhile in the east, it was assumed that the role of the sky dragons was to control all water, whether in rivers, seas, lakes, even wells, or as rain falling from the clouds. In addition they were believed to have created the stars. When angry, the sky dragons caused thunder and lightning; and as punishment to a people they could also declare a drought by 'gathering up' the waters of a region, bringing hardship to all.

In Wales, if rain fell on a funeral it was considered 'lucky' for the deceased, although no-one seemed to know the reason why, unless the heavens were weeping in sympathy. In other places rain usually symbolises sorrow; and sunshine, especially on a young bride promises glowing health and happiness for the future.

'It's raining cats and dogs' is a well known saying, although again, its origins are unknown. Most likely, it arose from the description of a downpour, when everything imaginable appears to be cast down from the heavens - among its many variations, pitchforks and shovels have been added! To say 'It's raining cats and dogs' could also apply to a person having a run of supposedly bad luck.

More subtle observations into the behaviour of birds and animals – whether wild or domestic – became an important source of weather-forecasting for the country dwellers of times past, especially during vital times like haymaking and harvest. For example, when a cat (particularly if black) washes behind or over its ears, it is an indication that rain is imminent or at least a change in the weather – this observation having been in common usage from around 1507 up to the present day. Again, if the cat sits with its back to the fire, this presages snow or frost or, more likely, rain. If high winds and storms are due, it is said the cat will chase its tail or even claw the furniture.

The larger birds, too, have offered their contribution to superstition. 'When,' it is said, 'the peacock loudly bawls, soon we'll have both rain and squalls.' Similarly, down on the farm, 'If the cock crows on going to bed, he's sure to rise with a watery head.' In Scotland, the frequent call of the cuckoo means a similar thing. So too, if fleas bite more than usual or pigs rush around the farmyard with straw in their mouths. Another indication of impending rain is when the rooks are sitting in rows on fences, walls or telephone wires. If the swallows fly low in summer, it indicates that this is where the air is dampest (thus attracting the insects which form their prey nearer to ground-level) – and means that rain could be near at hand. It is thought birds are very sensitive to atmospheric changes that precede rain – just as by contrast, the skylark will fly high up and sing when the weather is fine and dry.

Sailors, always deeply superstitious, believed that a cat was able to start storms by the magic stored in its tail. Accordingly, it was also said that such a feline friend was quite capable of taking on the guise of a witch, full of evil foreboding, so that the crew always made sure their ship's cat was well fed and contented. If it licked its fur 'against the grain' so to speak, a hailstorm was due. If it was playful, strengthening wind was nigh. And should it sneeze, rain would inevitably follow. On shore, as a measure of protection for their men folk, the sailors' wives often kept black cats at home, in the hope of guarding against storms and disasters at sea. In times of tempest, the women would even temporarily shut them away in the kitchen cupboard.

10 - Blessings from Heaven?

While global warming has been blamed for some areas of the world being overwhelmed by rain and other parts suffering from too little, the old term 'raining cats and dogs' has not always referred to heavy downpours of water. All sorts of things have mysteriously fallen from the skies, from Old Testament times to modern day. When the Israelites, led by Joshua, were pursuing the Amorites, great stones were cast down on the latter, forcing them to flee, with a great number of soldiers being killed. There have been other examples where non-meteorite rocks and stones have rained down from the skies. One theory is that they could have been ejected by volcanic activity, or swept up by whirlwinds. But cases where they have landed on specific places or targeted particular individuals more than once, put things in a very different category.

In ancient times, Kuju, a benevolent spirit of Yukaghir in Eastern Siberia, was said to have provided food to the inhabitants in the form of fish – so whenever fish appeared in huge numbers in the lakes of that region, they were believed to have fallen from the sky at Kuju's behest. Similarly the Greek historian Athenaeus wrote in 200 AD of a three-day deluge of fish and a similar fall of frogs, although the exact locations where this happened were not identified. Within more recent history there have been references to a storm of yellow mice that occurred in 1578 in Bergen, Norway. This, surprisingly, was followed by a shower of lemmings in the following year. In June 1809, the Natural History curator at Poitiers, in France got soaked in a violent rainstorm that included numerous small toads. Herring rained down in the Lorn district of Argyllshire, in 1821. The fish seemed to be of good quality and some were eaten by the local inhabitants. It is known that the nearby Loch Melfort is connected to the sea and herring, apparently, swim near to the surface. So could these have been somehow picked up by prevailing winds?

A yellowish substance that turned out to be edible fell in the Diyarbakir area of Turkey during August, 1890. The local people used it to make bread that tasted very good, and on analysis, it was found to be a form of lichen. The Book of Exodus reports how frequent rains of manna helped to sustain the Israelites during their time in the desert – one wonders if this, too, was a form of lichen. Other reports of strange 'rainfalls' have included less pleasant things like eels, stones the size of hens' eggs, seaweed, pitchforks, shovels – even flesh and blood! All these are very mysterious since, as they say, what goes up has to come down.

11 - Spooky Weather

After every case of 'February fill-dyke' we can rest assured that 'every cloud has a silver lining'!

Our forefathers placed their deepest beliefs in the sky and the heavens beyond, territories of the gods who wrought their wrath or beamed their approval on their subjects, according to whim. Major weather patterns are, on the whole, fairly basic and reliable – that is, they conform to the various seasons. But as we know, regardless of season, parts of a country may suffer inclement conditions while others get off comparatively lightly. This is becoming more and more likely to extend to continents as well – whether the fault of human beings for exploiting the planet, or possibly due to prophecies that the millennium would mark some kind of ending of the world as we know it.

But whether or not due to pollution and global warming, it is a fact that weather-wise, strange things have also happened in the past, backing up our forefathers belief that 'the gods' could be very restless and vengeful at times.

In July, 1949 a brief, but freakish blast of heat swept over several towns in Portugal. Although the phenomenon lasted only for a few minutes, the temperature rose from 100 degrees F to 158 degrees F. Many birds, including poultry, were killed and it was reported that several parts of the Mondego River dried up. During summer 1902, there were freak droughts and dust storms in Australia, the latter thick enough to seriously hamper navigation in the Malay Archipelago, blown all the way there by the trade winds. In 1880 an unusually sudden, ferocious thunderstorm struck Clarens, Switzerland. Thunder shook all the houses, and people working in a nearby vineyard saw a small girl, who was picking cherries, become enveloped in 'liquid electricity' as the tree was struck by lightning. People in a nearby cemetery found themselves enveloped in a luminous cloud. On touching each other they discovered sparks of electricity passed between them. But amazingly, neither they nor the small girl were harmed in any way.

Probably one of the most awe inspiring sights happened across European skies in 1750, when people witnessed great bows of light and strange, magnificent auras. There were many earthquakes over a vast area that year – including, in this country, London and Warrington – and these weird lights often preceded them. (My own theory is that they might have been gases burning in the sky, released from the earth by immediately preceding quakes). Again, in 1908 it was reported that the skies of the United Kingdom and Europe were brightly lit on 30th June and for several nights following. This was eventually put down to the infamous meteorite that exploded with gigantic force mid-air over the Tunguska area of Russia, where millions of forest trees were flattened, and people even 40 miles away suffered serious burns. By contrast, in April, 1904, the sky over Wimbledon went almost totally dark for 10 minutes. There had been no cloud or smoke worth speaking of – and certainly no eclipse of the sun.

12 - Mythical Beasts

By way of cave paintings, dreams, word of mouth and written record, Man has told many tales about mythical beasts. These, of course, never really existed; although many symbolise the meaning of good, while others represent evil. Those like the griffin, unicorn and dragon have been incorporated into heraldic design – and many commercial companies today incorporate a mythical beast in their logo. But there is always that fascinating hinterland where both myth and fact may occasionally rub shoulders.

Throughout the centuries, for instance, there have been innumerable reports of ships encountering huge sea-monsters. In 1724 while travelling to Greenland, a Norwegian missionary, Hans Egede (a reliable witness, one would assume), reported seeing such a monster raise itself so high out of the water that its head was 'above the mains'sol'. On its body, covered in hard skin, there were broad flippers and it had a long, pointed snout. The lower part reminded Egede of a large snake, the tail – when revealed – being the length of the entire ship.

In more recent times, there have been people who claim to have seen – even photographed and recorded the footprints of – the co-called Abominable Snowman, a man-beast believed to inhabit the more remote areas of America, the Canadian Rockies, Siberia and the Himalayas. There seem to be regional variations, however, regarding this ape-man. In Friston Park near Newhaven, Eastbourne, during the early hours of 18th November 2002, it is claimed that a lorry-driver, having parked in order to stretch his legs, witnessed a very large, human-like figure in the woods, lit up by a red lamp on some static forestry machinery. Moving closer, the lorry-driver shone a torch at the creature, which then ran off into the darkness while, suddenly panic-stricken, the man quickly retreated to the safety of his vehicle. Later he reported being unconvinced that the thing was human, for the powerful beam of his torch had not revealed normal skin-colour. The skin had appeared to be rather dull, indicating that the creature was covered by thick hair.

A possible earlier sighting is said to have happened in 1948, when a boy was rabbiting near some woods in the Horsham area. He described the creature he saw – by contrast – as a 2ft tall man covered in fur, with very long arms and pointed nose. Once it knew it had been seen, the creature also quickly made itself scarce. In both cases, might they simply have been apes 'on the run'? Or not!

There are also reports of a dwarf species living in Northumberland. And more elusive sightings of the much larger Yeti or Bigfoot – dating from the 1990s to the present day – come from the Midlands, especially the Cannock Chase area. In 2005 there were at least five reported sightings, although no photographs were obtained. But one wonders whether large, seven-foot mammalian bipeds would be able to survive on the meagre resources offered by British woods and moorlands. No bodies have ever been found – a fact accounted for by Charles Fort, the notorious collector of strange and wonderful tales, who once intriguingly suggested that they fade in and out of this time and dimension through some accident of metaphysics.

Just as mysterious is the large spectral Black Dog that is said to haunt the Nottinghamshire village of South Muskham. Unchallenged, it has been seen mainly by cyclists and walkers as it pads along Crow Lane towards Bathley, minding its own business. Many such creatures (known as 'Black Shuck' or 'Old Shock', 'Barguest', even 'Pooka', according to different localities) have been encountered throughout Britain. To actually see one is said to be an omen of death and they have been known to attack people in the past; but conversely, they may suddenly appear in a protective mode at the side of some vulnerable person (such as a woman travelling alone at night) only to vanish again once danger has passed. They are also known to haunt old graveyards, as well as country lanes, leaving no footprints behind.

Such spectral hounds – sometimes the size of a calf, or even bigger – are believed to be 'leftovers' from a pagan, pre-Christian Britain, a time when its inhabitants would have worshipped an assortment of gods, attended by their various dogs. The hounds are included in the Celtic legends of Arawn as well as in stories about the Viking god Odin, whose pack of baying hounds from Hell, with their large, saucer-like eyes of yellow or red, once viciously sought the souls of mortal beings.

13 - Supernatural Laws

The Supernatural World has baffling rules and regulations of its own. For example when Richard III, last of the Plantagenet kings, was defeated by Henry Tudor (ultimately Henry VII) at the Battle of Bosworth in 1485, we might have expected that it would be he who, in ghostly form, appeared on the battlefield still defending his kingdom – with, or without a horse! Yet it was not his ghost or that of the victor Henry Tudor who is seen, but those of two other people – one an ordinary soldier, but headless, the other a spectral horseman.

The ways of the supernatural promote much debate. Some people believe that the ghost of Henry VIII still shuffles pathetically around parts of Windsor Castle, clearly suffering from his ulcerated leg. Yet others feel that, despite being responsible for many terrible executions – including those of two of his wives, Ann Boleyn and Catherine Howard – the bloated, villainous king actually rests peacefully, caring little for the mayhem he caused. A supposedly unpleasant ghost usually reflects the character of the living person when they were making their mark on the society of their day - likewise the benevolent ghost is of someone who was kind and considerate towards the people he/she encountered during their lifetime. Although even this need not always be true.

There is the strange story of Mrs Sibell Penn, foster-mother to Henry VIII's son, the future Edward VI following the death of his mother Jane Seymour, of puerperal fever. The infection was the result of a Caesarean operation to ensure safe delivery of the child. Jane, alas, no longer important in Henry's eyes, realised she had been sacrificed for the sake of providing her dissolute husband with a male heir, death claiming her soon afterwards.

It was then that the King appointed Mrs Penn to do her duty towards his precious son. Well-liked, she excelled at her job, managing to remain in Henry's favour with the young Prince showing much affection towards her. When, at the age of ten, the boy himself became King, Mrs Penn found herself an important presence at Court. When he died at sixteen (of consumption) she was heartbroken, and mourned him as her own son. Subsequently she was rewarded with grace-and-favour rooms at Hampton Court Palace, where she was to die of smallpox in 1562.

Buried and honoured with an imposing monument in the old church of Hampton-on-Thames, so the worthy lady rested – until 1829, when the church was demolished and Mrs Penn's grave was disturbed, her monument being placed elsewhere in the present church on its completion. Her spirit thus roused, she was seen to manifest back in former territory – her rooms at Hampton Court. The then occupants began to complain of hearing angry mutterings, together with the rhythmic whirr of a spinning-wheel behind what was thought to have been a solid wall. When called in, the authorities discovered a secret door that led to a concealed room. Inside they found an old, well-used spinning-wheel, together with a collection of 16th century *bric-a-brac*. Old Palace records revealed that Mrs Penn had often used the spinning-wheel, lulling the sickly Royal child to sleep by its constant rhythm as she quietly sang to him. A small area of oak flooring had been worn away by the treadle.

Sibell Penn's ghost has often been sensed, especially by people staying overnight at Hampton Court Palace. Some having woken up terrified at feeling icy hands placed across their faces. Considering her highly thought-of disposition, the revenant could have been any one of numerous other ghostly spirits that inhabit the place – had it not been for the fact that some of the victims recognised the luminous ghostly grey figure of Mrs Penn leaning over them in a threatening manner.

14 - Fire Within

Normally the term 'fire within' can mean the potential energy within a person, a particular talent, something like integrity or a creative gift of some kind. Less positively we may come across or even unintentionally rouse the hidden fire, if we anger someone who has a deeply-seated temper. But I doubt whether many people have encountered anyone like Mrs Barbara Booley, whose temper literally started fires! Employed at the Berkeley Vale Hotel, Stone in Gloucestershire, a blazing row with the management saw her lose her job as cook in August 1971. Shortly afterwards an outbreak of fire occurred there.

In November another outbreak happened at St Hilda's School, Bridgwater, Somerset, where Mrs Booley had gained new employment. Again, the fire was claimed to have started following a row – and Mrs Booley moved on to the High School for Girls, in Bath. Easter 1973 saw the occurrence of yet another conflagration after a difference of opinion between her and a fellow employee. More fires broke out after she left another hotel in Tewkesbury, Gloucestershire, under a similar cloud. And the last one reported was during October 1975, after Mrs Booley was sacked from a job at the Torbay Hotel, Sidmouth, Devon. In every instance, when questioned by the police she strenuously denied responsibility but admitted that each blaze seemed to have happened following a heated argument. She was never charged, but expressed a wish she had been. Then, so she claimed, she would have been able to clear her name.

Of course there have been other similar cases. In 1982 Benedetto Supino, aged nine, from near Rome became known as a 'fire boy'. For a short period things like books, comics, even his bedclothes would burst into flames the moment he came into contact with them. Even furniture he happened to glance at, so it was claimed, would start to smoulder. Young Benedetto suffered painful burns himself at times. He was examined by doctors and physicists, but they failed to come up with any logical conclusions.

While working in Italy in 1983 Carole Compton, a young Scottish nanny, was tried for arson – accused of setting on fire a cot in which a three-year-old girl was sleeping. The previous night there had been an outbreak in the room belonging to the child's grandfather. Yet at the time of both fires, Carole had been dining with her employers. During her trial, it was revealed that she had become extremely dissatisfied with her employment and upset by an affair she had had with an Italian soldier. Her employer, Mrs Ricci, added that her two-year-old son also claimed that Carole burnt him each time she touched him. Although found guilty of arson and attempted murder, Carole Compton was later released and returned home to Aberdeen.

Possibly these cases (and many other examples) represent some kind of poltergeist activity, whereby an individual somehow attracts – usually unconsciously – a kinetic force that can cause havoc to people and property around them. Unhappiness, insecurity, even repressed sexual tension may be the cause. Thankfully, most of us do not attract such kinetic force – so the activities of 'fire-raisers' are fortunately very rare.

Nevertheless, there exists that strange, almost supernatural phenomenon referred to as Spontaneous Human Combustion (SHC). Not surprisingly, the very idea of a living person bursting into flames when there is no external evidence of fire - sometimes being reduced to a heap of ashes - has prompted fierce controversy for over 300 years.

More cases have occurred than official records indicate. In 1725, the husband of Nicole Miller of Rheims found her charred body still seated in an apparently unscathed armchair. Although he was convicted of her murder, good sense prevailed on appeal when it was realised that SHC had been responsible for her unexpected death. More recently, it was reported that a Cheshire lorry driver was discovered incinerated in his cab. The full fuel tank was found to be completely unaffected by the flames. At the inquest an open verdict was pronounced. In 1951, Mrs Mary Reeser of St Petersburg, Florida also died as a possible victim of SHC. In spite of very high temperatures, flammable objects in the same room as her body were left unscathed.

The medical profession may have been slow to recognise the phenomenon, but it has long been established that we all give off static electricity. For example, when we pull a pullover on over our head we can often hear the sound of crackling from our hair; if this is done in the dark, we may actually see fleeting, tiny sparks emitted. Dilys says that both healing and psychic energies are similar to electricity. In the same way that Mrs Ricci's young son claimed he received burns each time his Scottish nanny touched him, Dilys also reports that several times she has received a substantial electric shock when touching the hands of some of her clients. Electrical engineers are of the opinion that no such electrostatic discharge in the body is powerful enough to cause SHC. But tests on volunteers carried out by Professor Robin Beach in Brooklyn, USA, showed that readings ranged from those individuals who registered comparatively normal – to one woman who registered 30,000 volts.

There was a theory that a negative state of mind fed by illness, even loneliness, can induce the metabolism to produce certain chemicals called phostacens, which may build up in the body tissue. Such substances, it was claimed, were similar to nitroglycerine in that, under certain rare circumstances actual combustion may be induced. In 1980 in the *New Scientist*, it was also suggested that the anaerobic fermentation of food in the gut occasionally produces large amounts of flammable gas. Mixed with normal methane and hydrogen – and perhaps phosphorous dihydride – this could possibly account for the fatal incidence of SHC.

But although the phenomenon actually exists – many unfortunate victims providing evidence of it – and despite the wide medical knowledge on hand today, its true cause obstinately remains a mystery.

15 - Hallowe'en

Bonfires and burning effigies; children in masks and fancy dress waving pumpkin lanterns in the dark – these are the more familiar aspects of the Hallowe'en celebrations encountered nowadays. But what is the truth behind the acrid wood-smoke or the challenges of Trick or Treat?

The old Celtic year, being agricultural and lunar-based, concludes on October 31st – Hallowe'en, or All Saints' Day according to later Christian influences. The Celtic New Year begins on the following day (November 1st) also known as Samhain. One of the things the festival of this day marked was the insecurity of the coming winter, against which surplus livestock was slaughtered for food and sheep were mated to provide the following year's stock.

Samhain was also a time of cleansing, when great fires were lit to ensure the renewal of life in the earth after its long winter sleep. Fire also helped to keep away the wild beasts of the night and cleared any malevolent powers that might have been around at the darkest point of the year. These were represented by the burning of effigies, echoes from sinister times when live victims were sacrificed, both human and animal. Usually the effigy was that of a witch – once considered a convenient scapegoat for any suspicions a community might have held about anything questionable.

She, it was thought, could control the weather, fertility of the soil and the well-being of both cattle and humans. If the harvest had been good and the community healthy, all was well. If not, then retribution was demanded. When the Christian church, regarding witchcraft as some rival cult, attempted to rid itself of such opponents to the true faith, it adopted the same pagan style of ritual purification. Records of so-called 'trials' and inevitable punishment still make grim reading. Thousands of accused women were burnt at the stake.

In England of course, burning an effigy on the bonfire survives to this day. Instead of a witch, however, the effigy is that of Guy Fawkes and the custom has been moved to November 5th, when he and his accomplices (as we recall from school history lessons) plotted to blow up Parliament and the monarch James I on that date in 1605.

Hallowe'en or Samhain was also known as the Festival of the Dead when the physical and spiritual realms were supposed to come into close proximity, the dead being able to cross the threshold between the two worlds. Hence its reputation as ghostly and ghoulish, inhabited by 'things that go bump in the night'. It was believed that pumpkins, hollowed out and lit with candles, actually guided the spirits of the dead to where the mortal participants of the Festival had left food out for them. The origin of these lanterns was ancient Ireland, when hollowed-out beet and turnips would have been used. Later, when Irish immigrants settled in the United States they took the custom with them and used orange-coloured pumpkins instead.

So on any Hallowe'en the old pagan year dies, so the new one begins. *The wheel is come full circle,'* as William Shakespeare, as well as tradition, puts it. As we light our own pumpkin lantern or watch the display of celebratory fireworks round the bonfire, we might remember to say a quiet 'thank you' to the natural world for all the good things that have happened over the past year - and send out hopes for the mysterious and magical New Year ahead.

PART THREE
HAUNTED GROUND

8 THE STANDING PEOPLE

I have spoken to many individuals who readily admit to talking to trees, both in the woods and in their gardens. This might be regarded as eccentric, especially as the majority of people assume that trees cannot answer back and that they are 'just things', oblivious to human action or behaviour. We know dog and cat owners carry on long conversations with their pets, convinced the animals are responding accordingly – and gardeners who communicate with their plants also believe that they respond by showing exuberant growth and well-being.

So obviously there are hidden languages or communications that can exist between humanity and the various other forms of life in the natural world. Trees especially have always played a huge part in the daily life and welfare of mankind, exuding size and energy as they do. They have provided fuel, timber for protection and daily necessities as well as a 'feel good factor' and a sense of age and wisdom towards those who respect them, their longevity of life outweighing that of our own by far.

One cannot deny that something stirs the human soul whenever we become involved with woods, large or small, or catch sight of trees mysteriously silhouetted in groups along the skyline. Established street trees within an urban area can have the same affect; equally areas recently planted, particularly where young trees have begun to get established – drifts of oak, sycamore or birch. There are those who are convinced that trees communicate with, and care for each other. Our ancestors would probably have agreed. In fine weather, they believed these great giants rustled to each other in the breeze, while in stormy weather they would cry, shriek and roar against branch-cracking winds.

I have always found trees to be very spiritual, and over the years discovered myself many times to be communicating mentally with the trees and plants in my work as a horticulturist. This may have been how early man communicated with the trees that provided him with food (berries, fruit and nuts) as well as fuel and timber. Perhaps he would also have thanked the tree, in a similar way to the North American Indian who would thank the individual buffalo he was about to kill, for providing him with meat, and its skin for clothing.

The Native American Indians referred to trees as 'the Standing People' and venerated them as they did all things in nature. Encountered in large numbers such as a wood or forest they can be powerful and awesome, engendering a feeling of being watched by something mysterious, either among the trees or somewhere in ourselves. Tales and fables like those of the Brothers Grimm help to foster the reputation that the forest was a forbidding place good children were exiled to, or got lost in. In Spring, when the trees erupt into full leaf – following a long, dreary winter – we celebrate the English deciduous woodland as a thrilling, joyful, living thing – though with its contrasting moods, of course, - as well as its individual trees at different stages in their lives. At all ages, woods are still places of wonderful and fearful enchantment.

During the 11th century most of the population of England lived in clearings surrounded by thick forest, regarded even then as sinister – full of rumoured enemies, dangerous animals and marauding gangs of men. The country had once been tribal, consisting of small, squabbling kingdoms until Anglo-Saxon times; but by around 900 AD Britain had become united as one country (as I have mentioned earlier).

To our distant forefathers, the forest was an area of challenge, a hunting-ground, a source of fuel, and the haunt of the Green Man or Jack-in-the-Green; this long-time pagan deity of trees and forests – still respected today – was depicted in medieval churches as a combined man and tree. Such leafy areas were also the territory of other pre-Christian deities like the Romano-Celtic Arduinna, the Goddess of Forests and Hunting. Identified only from inscriptions and figurines in the Ardenne region, she is depicted riding a wild boar and is assumed to be the guardian deity of boars. The Romans identified her with Diana, their own Goddess of Hunting. Our woodlands still exude that strange feeling of mystery, whilst hosting a multitude of birds and animals, the nocturnal fauna in particular, like owls, bats, hedgehogs, and foxes with their weird, ghostly bark.

Woods and forests harbour many secrets, including that of shelter and protection to the likes of the legendary 'Robin Hood and his Merrie Men of Sherwode'. A whole host of stories, myths and legends awaits us when we enter the wildwood, the climax perhaps being in Shakespeare's 'Scottish' play when the usurper Macbeth receives news that Birnam Wood has in fact moved to high Dunsinane, and that his doom is upon him as the Three Witches had foretold. Renegades down the centuries found sanctuary here, as well as innocents who discovered that the harshness of the forest could be gentle and comforting.

Many dwelt in the forest through choice – solitary wise men and women or hermit-saints who lived out their lives of study and meditation in simple huts or caves; people would seek them out for their counsel and herbal cures. St Leonard, of St Leonard's Forest in West Sussex, is said to have slain a dragon during the 6th century, which had been terrorising the neighbourhood. During combat, however, he was wounded and the story goes that wherever the saint's blood spilt onto the forest floor, wild lilies-of-the-valley grew for the first time.

But Leonard had failed to rid the forest completely of its menace for in 1614, three men passing through claimed to have encountered 'a monstrous serpent', described as being about 9 feet in length, thick in its middle and thinner at each end; it had an underside of red scales, and similar, darker scales covering its back, with white ring-like markings encircling its neck. Its large feet, so it was reported, enabled it to run as fast as a man. Possible wing-cases were indicated as swellings on each side of its body. It was said to leave a trail of evil-smelling slime behind and could emit an accurate, but fatal spit, its victim, animal or human, immediately falling dead. Nothing more is known about what happened to this particular beast, although intriguingly, rumour of such creatures inhabiting St Leonard's Forest persisted well into the 19th century.

The Green Man of the forest appears in many guises, the god sprouting foliage and branches suggestive of the perpetual renewal of Life. Mysterious yet approachable, his effigies can still be seen in many of our cathedrals and churches, often carved *in situ* by stonemasons poised 20 metres (70 feet) high on precarious wooden scaffolding. By the 14th and 15th centuries, heads of lush foliage and branches were succeeded by heads suggesting death and decay, the population having been ravaged by the terrible Black Death. Leafy tendrils became worms that issued from mouths, worms that eased out eyes and teeth from their sockets, or represented roots of yew-trees that would ultimately penetrate every part of a body that rested in the churchyard. Decay was depicted indeed, but ultimate renewal too. Examples of these more dramatic effigies can be seen in Fountains Abbey, North Yorkshire; the church of Otterly St Mary, Devon, and the church at South Taunton, also in Devon, where the Black Death is believed to have first appeared.

The positive, more affable Green Man (though still a composite of both man and tree), reminds us of the legendary love between the god Apollo and the mortal Daphne. Following a row between Apollo and Cupid, the latter shot Apollo with a golden arrow, then shot Daphne with an arrow of lead. At once Apollo became smitten by an overwhelming love for Daphne who, overcome by rejection towards him, tried to escape but in vain.

Losing her strength, she prayed to the gods for protection and as Apollo stretched his hands out towards her, she was transformed into a laurel bush. His love for her was such that he adopted the laurel as his sacred tree, wearing a wreath of its leaves in her memory.

Such tales of love, happy or tragic, have often been portrayed against a woodland backdrop. What more appropriate setting for a romantic tryst, especially in the Springtime of year, than a thick canopy of leaves 'all freshe and grene', with pairs of lovers' initials boldly carved into the bark of tree-trunks – some tales go back centuries into the annals of folklore, or even into the mists of the supernatural - the trees themselves bearing wise and silent witness.

The old beliefs held that such trysts would have fared even better in a hazel grove, a place of kindly witchcraft and diverse blessings. The Druids regarded the **hazel** as the tree of wisdom and knowledge, fire, poetry and beauty; the flavour of its nuts particularly appealing to creative people and young lovers. Lucky forked hazel twigs were used to discover gold, as well as for water-divining, working with the natural energies of the land.

Everything has its own field of energy, trees and plants included. This has been proved by the use of a special photographic technique, Kirlian imagery, developed by Semyon Kirlian, a medical technician in Russia, during the 1930s. Using this technique the pictures of humans, animals, flowers, trees and leaves – even rocks – produce unique patterns of force similar to those shown by iron filings in close proximity to a magnet. A five or six-lobed leaf such as the sycamore or horse-chestnut, will show the original energy field even with one lobe missing. Likewise with someone who has lost an arm or a leg, the energy previously given off by the missing limb can still be shown as being present by means of Kirlian imagery.

More people regularly seek out the company of the Standing People than is realised in order to sort out their problems amid liberating, natural surroundings disturbed only by breeze and birdsong. Someone distressed or in mourning can spend time meditating amidst the trees, returning home greatly comforted. Basically, we rely on trees for gaseous interchange whereby they absorb the carbon dioxide which we exhale, one of their by-products through photosynthesis being oxygen, which they then release into the atmosphere for us to absorb, in order that we survive and prosper. But on a deeper level the interchange is significant in ways we cannot explain.

Where does this deep sense of communion between man and trees come from? Many English surnames reveal ancient family connections to individual tree species. Ashley, Birch, Oakley, Pine, Linden and Elder, for example, all stem from ancestors who had connections with these species, usually having lived near a group or a grove of them at some time in the past.

In much earlier times, man believed that the human race actually emerged from a tree – its size, the unfolding of its leaves and growing branches being symbolic of life itself. Thus tree-worshippers were very aware of the Universal Tree with its head in the heavens, its trunk close to the earth and its roots reaching far into the Underworld. There were also the closely-related **Tree of Life** and that of Knowledge. It was believed that the fruits from the Tree of Life were eaten by the gods in order to maintain their immortality. But such names were given to any majestic tree that thrived in a particular climate or area, with the result that a number of totally different kinds of trees shared the same names. These included *Ficus religiosa* of Hindustan and Ceylon, the Tree of Life under which the Buddha sat; the Universe Tree and the Tree of Life of India *(Asclepius acida)* and the Cassia Tree of Life from Southern China.

I once planted a small conifer *Thuya plicata (Arbor vitae)* – a Tree of Life – in my own garden. Within only a few years it had grown to a height of almost 20 feet and attained a magnificence that was entirely its own.

In Scandinavian mythology, the **Ash** tree is thought to be the origin of all living things, being referred to as the Yggdrasil, the World Tree, so vast that it was believed responsible for holding up the sky. The Greeks and Romans also believed the human race originally sprang from the Ash. The Greeks compared its shape to the images of clouds, and the nymphs that inhabited it as cloud goddesses. It is known that the Greeks also decided to adopt the oak tree as the original mother of the human race. It was believed that both the Tree of Life and the Tree of Knowledge grew in the Garden of Eden.

With its spirit of strength and wisdom the **Oak** has long been regarded as a holy tree and a lord of truth. From its leaves, the voice of Jupiter is said to have been heard. It was highly respected by the Druids, who also worshipped the rowan, believing that guardian spirits lived in these trees. Touching a tree was regarded as a mark of respect as well as for good luck.

Zeus was worshipped in a grove of oaks at Didona, in Epicuris. Here, his oracle oak was consulted by many, his response manifesting itself via the rustling of its leaves and branches or in the babbling of a nearby sacred spring. The magic was also maintained in pieces that had actually been severed from the oracle tree – one being incorporated as part of Jason's ship as a 'good luck' charm that provided the Argonauts with the vital knowledge needed for their epic voyage to seek the Golden Fleece.

9 TREES OF LEGEND

Time made thee what thou wast – King of the woods;
And Time hath made thee what thou art – a cave
For owls to roost in...

Yardley Oak
William Cowper

Individual trees as well as species have had legends, superstitions and beliefs build up around them in such a way that they form a huge part of our folklore and inherent sense of reality. When we 'touch wood for luck', we are unconsciously making direct contact with our distant forbears who actually worshipped the guardian spirits of the trees. After all, some trees are the longest-living things on Earth. Some specimens of yew for example, are known to be between 1,000 and 2,500 years old, while the North American conifer, the Wellingtonia, can reach surprising heights – some of over 300 feet – so is it any wonder that our ancestors regarded such living things as objects of worship? In Britain, the oak and rowan were worshipped by the Druids, who attributed great powers to them. When we do touch wood we are warding off not only misfortune but, according to our long-dead ancestors, we too are also paying our respects to the guardian spirits that lived in the trees.

Many of those early peoples believed that a huge tree was not only a source of profound wisdom but also represented the Earth's centre or a direct link between the heavens, earth and the underworld. This was certainly true of the Ceiba tree of Central and South America; while the holy Fig became associated with ancient fertility rites in India. The yew-tree, familiar throughout Britain, was considered sacred in many of the old European mythologies and because of its longevity it is still regarded by many as a symbol of everlasting life.

By contrast, in Nigeria it was the dead spirits of the Idem tribe who dwelled in one particular species of tree – and anyone who dared to fell such a specimen was doomed. Some Australian aborigines used to bury their dead within a circle of trees. Then a ring of bark was cut from each, creating a 'circle', thus trapping any possible spirits that might, in due course, have haunted the living.

Today there are many trees which have more modern, though still sinister connections. Near to Brampton in the Lake District, a monument marks the site where once stood an ancient oak-tree from which six rebels were hanged for their part in the 1745 Jacobite Rebellion. Records reported that their spirits 'were to be seen flitting about with airy ropes about their necks on each anniversary of the Day of Execution.' A similar tree that stood in Gallows Tree Lane in Upper Mayfield, near Ashbourne in Derbyshire retains connotations of immediate 'rough justice' similarly meted out to captured Jacobite soldiers, during their retreat from Derby as part of Bonnie Prince Charlie's Scottish army in 1745. Kevin, a Druid friend of mine, once came across a venerable tree which he felt had an atmosphere of deep sadness and depression around it. Enquiries revealed that this too had been used as a hanging tree, so the next time he passed that way, he put his arms round the trunk and blessed it.

Folklore suggests that to sleep under a tree helps to cure many ills. The elm tree was especially noted for its divine and medical properties and provided a living-space for good spirits. In medieval times, people would bruise the leaves and put them on wounds. That was not the case with one that once stood in Hyde Park, London, however - this was believed to be a very troubled, haunted elm. Vagrants warned against anyone thinking of spending the night beneath it because they would never wake up again. It happened that a gypsy called Black Sally ignored the warning and was found dead at sunrise, the next day. Thereafter it was always referred to as Black Sally's Elm. A number of people in the past had hanged themselves from its branches, and the resultant negativity that abounded was contrary to the wellbeing of the living. It was during the 1970s that the tree succumbed to Dutch Elm Disease and was finally cut down, although the feeling of negativity is still said to prevail on the site.

In my view as a horticulturist, the individual tree - like a human or animal 'loner' - may not always realise its full potential. I have seen lone specimens (say, of oak) looking sick, abandoned and 'stag-horned' – which means that the thick branches high up on the crown are dead. Trees of other species may also appear sick, the results of ploughing and fertilising being carried out far too close to the tree roots.

Spiritually, individual trees encountered in our daily round will still beckon, whether garden-based, seen on our way to work or encountered in the Park as part of a vital landscape; each is a tangible connection with the past. Some may still be quite young – little more than saplings – holding promise for the future; others could well be several times our own age, and considering their size and spirituality may have much to convey.

I once saw such large, mature oaks in woodland when travelling through Gloucestershire. What initially aroused my curiosity was the fact that they had been planted in rows, and I learned that they would have been used as timber to build the old 'wooden-walled' sailing-ships. With the introduction of metal-built craft, the original need for these particular trees has long gone.

Birkland Wood, Edwinstone near Nottingham, boasts the Major Oak, reported to be over 1,000 years old – which, thanks to expert preservation, is still growing. A modern tourist attraction, it was a focus of interest even in the 13th century: the trunk was said to have been thick and hollow enough to accommodate Robin

Hood and his men whenever the infamous Sheriff of Nottingham was known to be looking for them.

Another of Sherwood's legendary trees is the Parliament Oak. In the 13th century, while taking shelter beneath it, King John received news of a serious uprising by the Welsh. Together with his soldiers, he set out for Nottingham Castle where, in reprisal, he hanged a number of Welsh prisoners who happened to be incarcerated there. In 1290, whilst sheltering under the same tree on the way to Harby, Edward I's beloved Queen Eleanor was taken seriously ill. The king's counsellors advised him, nonetheless, to continue their journey and it was at Harby that the unfortunate queen passed away. The king and his retinue returned in deep mourning to London with her body, and 'Eleanor crosses' were set up in her memory at various sites where the procession halted.

It was to Boscobel Forest in Shropshire, that the young Charles II escaped, following the defeat of his army at the Battle of Worcester on 3rd September, 1651. Hidden high up in an oak-tree, he managed to evade the members of Cromwell's Puritan Army who were pursuing him. He finally escaped by night and thence to Europe and nine years of exile before the Restoration of the Monarchy in May, 1660. The oak has become synonymous with the Monarchy ever since, with Oak Apple Day once being celebrated on 29th May. A picture representing the King sitting in an oak-tree remains a well-known sign outside many public houses throughout the country.

As for the original Royal Oak, parts of it were hacked off by souvenir hunters over the years and by the 1890s it had met its demise. The present oak-tree on the site in Boscobel Forest is believed to have been grown from an acorn of the original tree.

Most sacred or healing wells, whose waters were believed to provide the cure for various human ailments, still have an all-important tree growing near them. This tradition may go back to times of ancient tree worship, for trees were as powerful as the wells were for water worship: or possibly it was the presence of such trees that was essential for a combined healing process to take place. In Staffordshire, the tomb of St Bertram at Ilam is in close proximity to the well named after him, and also to an ash tree. The beliefs of the ancients still linger, and may be considered as sacrosanct - the ash tree once being so venerated it was deemed extremely unlucky to damage it in any way. The same applied to other species of trees commonly found by wells - such as thorn, mountain ash, holly and yew. The Well of the Yew at Easter Rarishie (Ross and Cromarty) cured various ills so long as its tree-partner stood beside it. When the yew was cut down, the well was instantly robbed of its curative properties.

A spring known as Sul na Ba in the same vicinity, once flowed through a tree-trunk but eventually moved its position because, according to some pilgrims, it had felt misused. In Ireland, anyone who desecrated sacred trees by holy wells would suffer injury or even death as a result, while at Monzie, in Perth, a mineral well is said to have completely lost its powers in 1770, when two guardian trees fell of their own accord. Ailing visitors at many such wells would leave offerings such as pieces of clothing attached to a nearby tree or bush in the belief that as the cloth rotted, so their maladies would go into remission.

Legend tells of the thorn at St Mullen's Well at Listerling, Kilkenny growing from the original staff belonging to the saint after he had pushed it into the ground. Most sacred trees in Ireland share a similar story in folklore.

It is also believed that on a visit to Glastonbury, Joseph of Arimathea, accompanied by the Boy Jesus, drove a stake into the ground on Christmas Eve. During a short service he and his followers held, God responded by having the stake produce buds and ultimately grow into the tree which became known as the Glastonbury Thorn. This is famous for its flowering on or around

Christmas Day, in celebration of Christ's birthday. Cuttings taken from the tree have been known to prosper, although only a few inherited the Divine Gift of the parent tree which, when Glastonbury Abbey was built, was carefully transplanted by the monks to within its precincts. Shortly before writing this, I heard regretfully that someone had just tried to vandalise its successor.

10 THE FATE OF KINGS

The silver birch, a goddess tree, is symbolic of Lammas-tide, the 1st August. This important festival has celebrated from antiquity the harvesting of the corn, together with the first fruits, and the bounteousness of Mother Earth. Folklore decreed it a tree of Paradise, the emblem of everlasting summers in the world of spirit. It was also believed that the oak and birch were the equivalent of husband and wife for wherever the birch grew, so the oak would grow nearby.

The word 'Lammas' originates from the Anglo-Saxon *Hlafmas*, or 'loaf-mas', in recognition of the loaves which were made from the freshly-cut corn. But there is a more sinister meaning to Lammas-tide, which anciently refers to the seasonal death of the Corn King, spirit of the cornfields himself, which in pagan times was necessary in order to achieve a good harvest the following year.

According to Caesar and other Roman writers, the Celts – who had worshiped in forest groves and were rulers of Britain for approximately 500 years before the Roman invasion – actually performed human and animal sacrifices as offerings to their gods as part of the various festivals they celebrated. The cult film *The Wicker Man* portrays animals and a modern human sacrifice being burned alive in a wicker framework representing a huge 'man', while the pagan inhabitants of 'Summerisle' sing the old folk tune *Summer is Acumen In*. Despite the advent of Christianity, various aspects of paganism were to survive for a very long time, including the old belief that in order to attain something a sacrifice had to be offered in return.

One historical example of this might have been the dramatic death in the New Forest of William II of England. The event occurred early in the evening of 2nd August, 1100 when William

Rufus (so-called on account of his red face) died in a clearing in the forest immediately after being struck by an arrow.

He and his seven companions, each armed with bow and arrows, had been strategically positioned among the trees as the chief huntsman instructed the beaters to drive two stags into the clearing. The king took aim and shot. Because the sun was in his eyes, he merely grazed the first animal which retreated quickly back into the thicket. Then, so the official story goes, Walter Tyrrel, one of the company, shot at the second stag and almost achieved a hit – the arrow quickly deflecting from off the animal's back, straight into the king's heart.

Aghast, the friends considered the situation. Had it been an accident – or something more sinister? The fatal arrow was one of a new set the king had given Tyrrel at the start of the day's hunting, but Tyrrel emphatically denied he had been in any strategic position to have taken deliberate aim at the king. Realising that he might be the main suspect if the king's death was treated as murder, he quickly mounted his horse, departed for Poole and sailed for Normandy. The rest of the company quickly decided to disappear, leaving William Rufus's body where it lay.

Two hours later, according to ecclesiastical accounts, the body was discovered by a charcoal burner who wrapped it with a ragged cloak, dumped it on his rough cart and took it to Winchester, a journey of about 20 miles. It was said that the king's blood nourished the earth wherever it spilt along the route (in a similar way to St Leonard, whose fatal wounds dripped blood causing lilies-of-the-valley to grow wherever it touched the forest floor).

If Tyrrel did not kill the king, whether wilfully or by accident – and a number of accounts at the time supported his innocence – then who did let loose the fatal arrow? Suspicion points to a planned assassination by William Rufus's younger brother, Henry, so was it he who bribed someone to carry out the deed? When the body reached Winchester the next morning, Henry appeared to be suspiciously upbeat and by mid-day the corpse of William Rufus had been buried. By the afternoon, Henry had rushed off to London to be crowned as Henry I before Robert, his elder brother, was legitimately able to claim the throne.

According to the historian Duncan Grinell-Milne, the situation was clear. At the time William Rufus died, Walter Tyrrel was an estimated 80 yards away from the king, which meant that he could not have got a clear aim with his bow because of the trees. It is believed that whoever did let loose the arrow must have been very much nearer to where the king stood at the edge of the clearing, to achieve the fatal shot. Could it have been the head huntsman?

The official story that Tyrrel's arrow glanced off the back of the second stag and was deflected into the king's heart, does not hold up. Under the circumstances, having lightly engaged with the animal, the arrow would have gone harmlessly into the ground. Another version of what happened was that, having only slightly wounded the first stag and with his hand shielding his eyes from the bright sunlight, William Rufus, with bow and arrow, pursued the animal as it retreated into the thicket. Meanwhile Tyrrel aimed at the second stag, let loose his arrow and struck the king.

And whether it was an accident or a planned assassination, there was another possible explanation for the death of William Rufus. Was the official (ecclesiastical) version a Christian cover-up to conceal the real story – that a ritual pagan sacrifice was being made? William Rufus had been to all intents and purposes, a pagan king. His contempt towards Christianity had been well known. During his reign he had even plundered the Church and other religious establishments. A favourite oath he used was 'By the Face of Luca!' which anthropologist Margaret A. Murray suggests in her book *The God of the Witches*, is the Latinised version of Loki, the name of one of the original gods of the Norsemen. Over time and with the adoption of new ideas, the god Loki would have become regarded as the Enemy, or the Evil One (the Devil) in the eyes of expanding Christianity.

Alternatively, 'By the Face of Luca!' could have been a corruption of the name of the Irish god Lugh, after which the lunar-orientated Celtic Festival of Lughnasa (the equivalent of Lammas-tide) is named. William Rufus indeed came from pagan stock, still showing support for the 'Old Religion' despite the fact that his father William I and Henry, his brother, were Christian.

The pagan religion was still comparatively widespread among the ordinary people, so it is likely that they would have welcomed William Rufus in succession to his father – the hated Christian king William the Conqueror who had devastated the land and eliminated the Anglo-Saxon system. To the pagans, William Rufus was their own god-king, though what has come down to us about the man survives mostly through ecclesiastical accounts of the day, biased against him because of his beliefs. According to the Church's annals, he was buried hurriedly at Winchester being, significantly, denied the last rites. The date of his death (2nd August) was also significant, since it was known as 'the morrow of Lammas' – the pagan day after the Lammas-tide Harvest Festival – a traditional time for human sacrifice to be offered to the gods.

The sacrificial victim, as with all offerings to the gods, needed to be as perfect as possible. So the practise of sacrificing the king (the Divine Victim) in his prime, before his natural strength had began to abate, was an obvious precaution to ensure that all would be well with the harvest and the world, his blood being offered back to enrich Mother Earth in thanks for her bounty. Sometimes the king's son would be offered as a sacrifice instead, although it was necessary for the king to indicate that the death of his son would equally serve the purpose his own death would have done. As the king was fated to die in place of the god, so the son would die in his stead, being equally invested (temporarily) with the divine attributes of his father.

There is more evidence to back up this tale of pagan sacrifice. On the previous May Day Eve, William Rufus's young illegitimate son had mysteriously died. Rumour had it that he had offered himself in his father's place; but the gods of the Old Religion had still demanded the sacrifice of the Divine Victim himself. It is believed that William Rufus knew that he was the One who would be called upon to offer his life, and was also aware that he was about to die on the day he did – 2nd August – a fact that was known over a wide area before it happened. After the event, news had spread to the Continent within hours.

Norman poets (who also may quietly have been of the Old Religion), wrote their own version of the discovery of his body in the New Forest, its transportation to Winchester and of the grief shown by various noblemen – and even some bishops – as the dead king was placed on a bier and covered with a great mantle. Despite the ecclesiastical writings against William Rufus, the monk Ordericus Vitalis recorded that many of the poor folk, men, widows and orphans gathered to join the funeral procession to the hastily arranged burial. This showed that he had been held in high regard by them; in fact they were pagan believers bidding farewell to their sacred God-King.

Once the king's body had been placed on the charcoal-burner's cart, it is said that the royal blood continued to drip (an indication of murder in itself, according to folk-belief) and nourished the earth. The waters of Ocknell Pool are said to turn red on the anniversary of his death, either because his body was carried past the spot or because Walter Tyrrel washed his blood-stained hands there, while making his escape. The ghost of William Rufus continues to follow the route from the Rufus Stone, set amid the peacefulness of the New Forest, all the way to Winchester.

It was William the Conqueror and his successors who brought in savage laws to protect the deer in the New Forest. William Rufus himself had introduced maiming and hanging as punishment for any commoner found poaching. Even for disturbing the deer, they risked having their eyes put out. Further stories based on the gruesome killing of William Rufus were chronicled by ecclesiastics such as William of Malmsbury (1128) and Geoffrey Gaimar (c.1140).

Some years before, an old man whose dwelling had been demolished on the orders of William the Conqueror when the New Forest was cleared for hunting purposes, laid a curse on the king's sons, prophesying that they would die in that location. So was it in fulfilment of the curse that not only did Rufus die there, but Richard, his younger brother, was gored to death by a stag? Certain members of the clergy claimed to have dreamt that William Rufus, following a violent death, would go to hell, and one monk actually approached the king to tell him about his dream. But interestingly, it is reported that the monk was ridiculed and given one hundred shillings to go on his way. Was the king increasingly disturbed by reminders of a gruesome fate in store for him? Was he a willing sacrifice, or did he hope to avoid his violent demise? It was later claimed that on the night before his death, he himself had a vivid nightmare whereby a surgeon was drawing his blood to such an extent that it flowed into the sky, to partially obscure the sun.

According to Matthew Paris (1200-1259) a close friend of the king, Robert, Earl of Moreton, whose land covered Bodmin Moor in Cornwall, claimed to have been approached on the moor one day by a terrible apparition. It was of a large black goat carrying on its back a body, naked, blackened and pierced through the heart. The shaken Robert ordered the goat to tell him who he was carrying and the reply was: 'I am carrying your King in judgement!' The ghostly messenger added that a spirit had been sent 'at the bidding of St Alban who complained to God of him, to wreak vengeance on Rufus for his oppression of the English Church.'

The goat vanished, and shortly afterwards the Earl learned that the king had been slain at the very moment he had encountered the phantom.

But despite the ecclesiastical chronicles condemning him outright as an evil heathen king, William Rufus was a man of his time; a man of fierce conceit, a man capable of both fair and very harsh justice. He was honourable in his way, but determined; a fighter who was sometimes unnecessarily ruthless. But these were the qualities of a pagan God-King.

SUPERNATURAL SNIPPETS No 3
Haunted Ground

16 - The Spectral Hunter

All woods and forests should be treated with the same reverence and sacredness as when we enter a church or cathedral. After all, man's original inspiration for those massive stone pillars built for the glory of God, were the trees themselves. Should we go blundering into the leafy kingdom, the trees might conspire against such irreverence – and unexpected happenings occur.

On a night during the early 1960s, a group of youths, so it is said, found an old hunting-horn at the edge of a clearing in Windsor Great Forest. As they laughed, joked and fooled around, one of them put it to his mouth and blew. Almost immediately they heard the call answered from a distance. At first, they thought it was nothing more than an echo. But the joking stopped when they heard what sounded like a pack of wild, baying hounds fast approaching, which burst into their field of vision led by the spectral figure of a man festooned with chains and dressed in animal skins, mounted on a huge black horse, heading straight towards them. This was Herne the Hunter, legendary leader of the ghostly Wild Pack – his hunting-horn draped around his neck, his bow and arrow at the ready – recognisable by a great pair of antlers on his head silhouetted against the moon.

Herne is seen regularly in Windsor Great Park, especially in times of national crises. He was originally a royal huntsman who is said to have once thrown himself between a wounded stag and the king, thus saving the king's life though he himself was mortally wounded. A wizard suddenly appeared and told the king that the only way Herne's life could be saved was by cutting off the stag's antlers and tying them to his head.

This done, Herne recovered and for a few years he was the king's favourite. Inevitably other huntsmen became jealous and plotted against him; and convinced by their untruths the king dismissed Herne who ultimately committed suicide by hanging himself from one of the many oaks in Windsor Great Park - one of the areas where his spirit has been seen is the Long Walk. But which tree was actually 'Herne's Oak', no-one knows precisely. In his volume titled *Arboretum Britannicum*, published in 1838, John Loudon tried to identify two likely possibilities, although both were completely dead even in his day and cannot now be traced.

Another version tells us that Herne was Warden of the Park, but under which king – Richard II, Henry VII, or Henry VIII? Again, we do not know. It is said that he chose to kill himself rather than stand trial, accused of witchcraft. There have been many variations on the story, even by Shakespeare, who mentioned Herne in *The Merry Wives of Windsor*.

Herne is identified with Cernunnos, the Horned God, probably the earliest of male deities. He is seen portrayed in 16,000-year-old cave paintings both in France and Spain, depicted as a dancing goat-horned figure or as a man wearing antlers of a stag and deer skin. Part Nature, part man, his identity became fused in the belief of his followers as both hunter and hunted.

Such a deity would naturally have evolved around Stone Age hunting communities who, through the bitter cold of successive Ice Ages when vegetation was at a premium, depended largely on wild animals for food.

To the Celts, horns and antlers became highly symbolic of virility and fertility; this particular Celtic god Cernunnos, representing both, was worshipped from prehistoric times to approximately 1,000 AD, and is thought to have originated from Central France. He was also a god closely associated with animals, rather than representing an animal spirit; and as the Horned God was capable of taking on the form of any animal his worshippers might have wished for. Interestingly, Cernunnos is depicted on the Gundestrup Bowl from Denmark in the company of a boar, an animal highly respected by the Celts for its wildness and warrior potential which was used to invoke the ferociousness needed to terrify their enemies. The boar's image was also depicted on bronze shields, swords and helmets, to create the power and magical properties essential for protection in battle.

On the same bowl the god is also seen in association with a bull, another sacred animal. In Britain the Celts were keepers of cattle, central to their way of life, the number owned indicating the degree of wealth. Health, wellbeing of the herd and of the family and the production of children, were paramount for survival. Bulls that had been castrated, as oxen, pulled the plough, cart and drew water. Bronze horns and rattles were used in Druid ceremonies to call the spirits, inducing awe in those taking part to celebrate the sacredness of the bull. The power and profundity of the animal was equated with Taranis, the thunder god of Romano-Celtic belief. To the Romans he was on a par with Jupiter, although, like Arduinna, the Goddess of Forests and Hunting, he is known to us only through a small number of inscriptions, one being identified at Chester. His symbol is a spoked wheel; as a god he demanded savage rites.

A stone relief discovered at Cirencester depicts Cernunnos associating with snakes. He is also depicted elsewhere with his legs replaced by snakes. A relief was found with the god in the company of an unknown goddess holding a basket and feeding a snake. Symbolically, the snake represents rejuvenation. Other reliefs show Cernunnos holding money purses.

As for the youths who unwittingly summoned the phantom of Herne the Hunter in Windsor Great Park, when faced with the spectre of the god and his strange forces, they dropped the old hunting-horn and fled the scene as fast as they could.

17 - Ghosts in the Garden

Fine weather beckons us all out into our gardens, regardless of their size. Yet gardens may turn out to be hotbeds of mystery and ghostly intrigue. Many scandals, even plots, have actually been spawned in the open air, to avoid those ever-listening walls and secret passages, complete with spy-holes which can threaten privacy indoors. Thomas Percy once held the lease of Baddesley Clinton in Warwickshire, a medieval manor house surrounded by a moat. The atmosphere vibrates with eerie presences from a past that no longer exists. Or does it? It was here that Percy's friend Guy Fawkes once also lived, and they were two of the men who played prominent roles in the treasonous Gunpowder Plot. In the fine walled garden, male ghostly voices have been heard arguing and it is said that the sound of weird footsteps are also encountered. Shadowy forms have been seen and, some years ago, a former administrator confronted a spectral soldier in the same area. Judging by his uniform, he was thought to be from the time of Waterloo.

At the 19th century mansion known as The Binns, in West Lothian, Scotland, the ghost of General Tam Dalyell has been seen flamboyantly riding his white horse through the grounds. More intriguing is the figure of an old man occasionally spotted gathering firewood. Incredibly, he is believed to be the ghost of an ancient Pict. A more dramatic story concerns the lovely young woman often observed in the beautiful garden during daylight hours, near to the keep of Scotney Castle, Lamberhurst in Kent. She is believed to have been betrayed in love at some time, and in her despair created a great outcry of hysterical grief. In order to silence her and avoid attention, she was mysteriously killed and her mortal remains hidden in a secret rocky area – ironically, the very place where she and her lover used to meet.

In November 1945, the Camp Hill area of Leeds saw many rows of old terraced houses being demolished. Stripped of their doors, floorboards and window-frames, some provided dubious areas of adventure for local school-children, a group of whom were busily exploring the vicinity one day, by jumping from joist to joist on the upper floors and staring down through the window gaps at the masses of smashed bricks and timber below. One boy named Peter Turner was puzzled as he looked down on what seemed to be a small, well-cultivated rose-garden in full bloom, despite the wintry season, being lovingly tended by an old man. But Peter's immediate concern was whether he had been discovered trespassing in such an unsafe area, so he called to his friends to run for it in case the old man reported them. It was not until afterwards that the impossibility of a secret garden existing amid such dereliction actually occurred to the boy.

Despite a subsequent search among the mounds of rubble – even below the very window-gap he had originally looked through – Peter was unable to find any sign of the beautiful garden, which of course, none of his friends had seen. We are all psychic to a greater or lesser extent, and he may have experienced some sort of time-slip to a bygone era, when there could have been a beautiful rose-garden there in place of the small backyard more usual of a terraced property. Or the garden could even have existed in an earlier era before the terrace of houses itself was constructed. Sometimes there can be several layers of haunting in the same place with ghosts materialising from different time frames.

18 - The Earliest Ghost

One of the oldest reported ghost appearances was written down by Pliny the Younger, who lived in Rome during the first century AD. Like his uncle Pliny the Elder, he was renowned for his care and accuracy in recording what he heard and saw, especially with regard to everyday life in Rome at that time. Although Pliny was not a particularly superstitious man, he seems to have been very impressed by what he had been told and was ready to vouch for the accuracy of the following story, which he wrote in a letter to his patron, Lucias Sura.

There was a large, spacious house that once stood in Athens, with a reputation for being badly haunted. Witnesses reported that in the dead of night loud moans had been heard, as well as the clanking of chains which grew louder, before the grim spectre of an old man appeared. Tall but bent over, he was a picture of woe and filth, with dishevelled white hair and a dirty, matted beard. As he staggered forward, the witnesses saw his thin legs were shackled by chains. Likewise his wrists were bound with long, heavy links, which rattled profoundly whenever he shook his arms in fury. It was said that some of the witnesses had died of fright at seeing such a wretched sight – or some died later of disease, the property being thought of as cursed.

The house was put up to rent, and stood empty. It gradually began to show signs of decay as years passed, with nobody showing any interest in living there. That was until Athenodorus, the philosopher, arrived in town. Short of money, he was looking for a small place to rent - and was curious about the low rent required for such a large property. On enquiring, he was told openly about the spectre – and the philosopher decided to take on the house regardless. A creature of habit, Athenodorus would work in his study late into the night, calculating his philosophical thoughts and writing them down. Inevitably, the sound of rattling chains gradually became more and more audible, but Athenodorus chose not to be interrupted in his work. Eventually, he was shocked to see the ghostly figure manifest itself before him, but unlike the hysterical witnesses, he did not panic. Instead the philosopher simply indicated with his hand that the ghost was disturbing him and should go away.

Each night the same thing happened and it was a question of who would give way first. The spectre persisted in moaning and clanking his chains even more loudly. The philosopher grew more and more impatient at being interrupted, until at last, he sighed heavily then rose, picked up his lamp and indicated to the spectre that if it would lead the way, he was prepared to follow. It glided before him – through the house and out into the garden. There it approached a spot near a large shrubbery, where it nodded to the philosopher and then vanished.

The next morning Athenodorus approached the authorities and reported his experience, suggesting that the spot where the spectre had disappeared should be investigated. After digging not far below the surface, to everyone's surprise, a human skeleton bound in ancient, rusted chains was discovered. Having obviously been interred hurriedly at some time, the remains of the chained man were collected together and eventually given a burial in the proper manner. Whatever the status of the man – whether slave or prisoner – and however he had come to perish, his phantom was obviously satisfied; the house was never troubled by bad luck or ghosts again.

Perhaps this is the archetypal story – the sceptic's view of what a ghost is – simply something that does little but moan and rattle chains. But those with a respect for the paranormal know otherwise. According to Greek mythology, it was customary to ensure that the spirits of the dead rested easily, since they would have no need to trouble the living if their bodies had been properly buried. So the Greeks, together with other ancient civilisations, went to considerable lengths to see that their dead were respectfully interred. Even in our own, highly scientific age, the strenuous efforts made to recover the bodies of the dead (whether through the result of accident or war) go back partly, to the old suspicions that the spirit of an unburied person may return to harass the living.

Dilys reports how she was initially rather sceptical about the importance of traditional burial, but over the years she has worked as a medium, she encountered an increasing number of cases where the spirits of the dead made contact to express their wishes about the disposal of their bodies. One young man who had committed suicide had been cremated, and he told Dilys how much he wanted a 'proper' grave with a gravestone and flowers laid – he even described the type and colour of the flowers – dark pink carnations. Dilys has told me that recently departed spirits often reveal how much they are looking forward to their funerals; and I have heard the same reported by other mediums.

19 - Haunted Ally Pally

'As the figure in blue overalls approached along the tunnel, members of the night maintenance team were terrified on seeing the look of sheer horror on its face as it was about to disappear into the tunnel wall.'

This occurrence happened regularly on the London Underground, near to Moorgate station, while workmen were employed on adapting the Great Northern and City Tube tunnels during the winter of 1974-5. The spectre was assumed to be that of a maintenance worker who was killed by a train some years before on that section of the line. Following the Moorgate rail disaster in February 1975, it was thought that the same apparition may have caused the train driver's concentration to lapse during vital seconds before the crash. It has also been suggested that the spectral appearance at that particular moment may have been a premonition of the disaster.

Something equally as sinister may have had a long term affect on the fortunes of Alexandra Palace which was built on a hill between Hornsey and New Southgate in the 1860s. The site had originally been a gypsy encampment and when they were evicted for building to begin, the gypsies laid a curse, pronouncing: 'May death and destruction befall this place and everything associated with it.'

'Ally Pally', as it became known, was famous as a major venue and particularly on account of its grounds, but within days of its opening in 1873 it was destroyed by fire and had to be rebuilt. Its subsequent history was a catalogue of disasters that earned it the reputation of being a 'white elephant'. Plans for a major relaunch were announced, but the 'Old Pally' was again destroyed by fire in 1980.

Originally, a line from Finsbury Park via Crouch End, Highgate, then through Muswell Hill to Alexandra Palace was built. Later London Transport planned an electrified extension of the Northern City Tube from Archway, taking in Moorgate, to the venue. As a result, the station at Highgate was rebuilt in 1941 but due to the austere times following World War Two, the extension was never fully completed, and the station eventually closed, its tracks being taken up in 1971.

Situated in a deep cutting, partially concealed by thickets of trees and bushes, with tunnels at either end, an eerie atmosphere presently engulfs the beleaguered station. The ghost of a man who committed suicide in the early 20th century by walking into the path of an approaching steam train in one of those tunnels, is said to haunt the place; while people living close by claim to have heard the sounds of phantom trains in the tunnels, and passing to and fro through the station at night.

Those curious-minded enough to climb down to the weed-infested platforms in daylight, have reported an overwhelming feeling of being watched by souls from long past. Perhaps they might not all be those who used the station in its day. Other revenants could well be the souls from the original gypsy encampment, taking their revenge – it was their curse, perhaps, that caused the Moorgate disaster of 1975.

20 - The Spectral Light

Because of where they are located – along wild shore-lines and isolated, rocky islands – many lighthouses have provided a background to a myriad of strange, eerie stories. In December 1900, for example, the supply ship *Hersperus* was approaching Eilean Mor, an island off the Scottish west coast, with relief lighthouse-keeper Joseph Moore on board. Moore had become increasingly concerned because the lighthouse there had been dark for eleven days.

A thorough search by the ship's crew revealed that, although deserted, everything had been left in impeccable order, except that bad-weather gear belonging to two of the three keepers was missing. It was suggested that all three had been swept away during a recent storm that had also damaged the jetty below. Yet would three such experienced men, in their right minds, have even approached the jetty – damaged or not – during such terrible weather? Another theory was that because of their isolation, they might have had a fatal argument; could one of the keepers have 'cracked' under the strain and run amok, despite the efforts of his two companions to restrain him? No bodies were ever found.

On a small island named Lady Elliot off the Great Barrier Reef, Australia, a wood and iron lighthouse was built during 1873. One of the early keepers employed there was Thomas McKee, who had brought his family from Ireland with the promise of a better life in their new country. But the island, with its cottage and nearby small burial-ground, proved anything but hospitable. His wife Susannah yearned constantly for a life elsewhere away from loneliness and danger. Her desperate pleas fell on the deaf ears of her husband, so much so that in April 1907 she put on her best dress and threw herself into the sea; her body being recovered next day by Thomas, who buried her in the tiny cemetery. Despite rumours that he had wilfully drowned her, nothing in that respect was ever proved.

It was some years later that Arthur Brumpton, another lighthouse keeper, and his daughter encountered the spectre of a woman walking between the cottage and the lighthouse. They were to see her on a number of occasions, sometimes wandering further afield during their stay on the island, although they could not identify her. In 1940, when the Brumptons were on board ship heading back to Brisbane, the Captain showed them photographs of some former inhabitants of Lady Elliot Island. To their amazement, they recognised one as the spectre they had encountered – that of Susannah McKee – still wandering there despite the inhospitality of the place.

For a long time, the treacherous rocks at the entrance of Boothbay Harbour, Maine, USA had spelt doom for many vessels. Around 1800, fishermen began placing a lighted lantern on the rocks at night to warn other crews of the impending danger. This proved to be of less help to larger vessels, but certainly aided the smaller craft belonging to fellow fishermen. Then, inexplicably, there began to appear the alarming spectral figure of a 'woman in white' on wild, roaring nights – flamboyantly waving a flaming torch while standing on the reef. At other times her luminous figure was seen standing in a burning vessel, frantically waving her arms in the air. Occasionally, she was even accompanied by lightning! Yet the many ships and men taking heed of her warnings were saved from certain disaster offered by the ever-present rocks.

It was not until 1883 that the US government decided to build a lighthouse. But to this day, there are people who claim to have seen the figure of the ghostly woman in white (her origins being veiled in mystery) still watching the entrance to Boothbay Harbour. On standby, should the lighthouse 'go dark' perhaps?

21 - Auld Reekie

The Scottish people were in the news during September 2014 regarding their historic decision to remain a part of the United Kingdom. But Scotland has its own mysterious history, especially its capital city Edinburgh – brightly alive during the summer months of its annual Festival, but with a hidden dark side. 'Auld Reekie', as it is more familiarly known, has a well-deserved ghostly reputation.

In Charlotte Square, a phantom coach has been seen as well as the apparitions of an 18th century woman, together with a ragged beggar and a monk – their origins being unknown. More sinisterly, persistent bloodstains on certain floorboards in Holyrood House are connected to David Rizzio's grizzly murder in 1566. Secretary to Mary, Queen of Scots, his ghost as well as Mary's, has been witnessed from time to time. Meanwhile, from the Esplanade of Edinburgh Castle the spectre of a headless drummer beats a slow, unfamiliar rhythm. Thought to date from the mid-17th century, he may have been connected with the Civil War, when Cromwell's forces reached Edinburgh in September 1650 and surrounded the castle. Following a siege lasting three months, the Governor, Walter Dundas and his men had no option but to surrender.

Then there was Major Thomas Weir, a charismatic lay-preacher of the Presbyterian Church and Commander of the City Guard, who was burned at the stake on 11th April, 1670. His sister Grizel was hanged in the Grassmarket the next day. This was a notorious case. Not only having confessed from the pulpit to having made a

142

pact with the Devil, Weir apparently also admitted to having had an incestuous relationship with his sister and sharing with her in the knowledge and practice of witchcraft and satanic rituals. Their house was finally demolished in 1878, since it was believed that ghostly and sexual parties still occurred there; the Major's spirit, wearing a sheet of fire and riding a headless black horse, is still seen galloping towards West Bow, while the apparition of his sister reveals her having been blackened by the flames of Hell.

Closer to our own time, the basement to the High Street Police Station was once used as a mortuary. Working there was a large, burly attendant who was very interested in American comics. Even when wearing his large white apron in the performance of his duties, he made sure his favourite form of reading was somewhere nearby. Although as part of his job he was allocated an office, he far preferred seeing to his charges amid the quietness of the mortuary, sometimes spending his breaks in there with a comic in one hand and a mug of tea in the other. Following years of service in the job he loved, he was discovered dead (of a heart attack) in the mortuary one night; later, it was reported that a large familiar figure in a white apron had been sighted there – maybe on a more permanent break – with comic in one hand and mug of tea in the other. Obviously he still loved his job and was anxious that it should be done properly by others.

The sad story of Angus Roy, a merchant seaman from nearby Leith, began when in 1820 while at sea, he fell from the ship's mast. Although badly injured, he survived but was forced to live out the rest of his life in Edinburgh's Victoria Terrace. With one leg virtually useless, dragging behind as he limped through the dark narrow streets, he was targeted by local children who teased and tormented him for years, so much so that the unfortunate man vowed to have his own back on those who had caused him so much grief. He died in 1840, but his alarming spectre, dragging his useless leg behind him along Victoria Terrace, is reputedly still seen and heard, terrifying both children and grown-ups alike.

These are just a few of the city's supernatural stories for 'Auld Reekie', with either pride or shame, does not allow us to overlook her grim legacy.

22 - Wild Edric

Is it possible that a folk-hero like Robin Hood never existed, in spite of being such an inspirational icon to England's oppressed peasantry battling against medieval injustice? We might ask the same question about Wild Edric, whose presence amid the remote area of Minsterley, in Shropshire is still felt today. A folk hero of many unusual legends, it is hard to identify the real man behind the myth. Born Edric Salvage in 1035 at Weston under Redcastle, his estates within the West Country are mentioned in the Domesday Book – so he must have existed. After the death of King Harold Godwinson at Hastings in 1066, the new Norman rulers quickly imposed a harsh regime of floggings and hangings. When he protested to William the Conqueror about the viciousness of so-called Norman justice, Edric was given short shrift, so he and his followers determined on rebellion from the Welsh Marches.

Ravaging the countryside, they then attacked the Norman garrison in Hereford, and eventually sacked Shrewsbury in 1069. Pursued by the savagery of William's army, Edric was forced to seek hiding in the wilderness of Long Mynd. It was here that, according to folklore, he married Lady Godda, his beautiful elfin bride, thus obtaining the protection of the fairy folk in this forested area.

Edric continued to pursue his acts of rebellion against the Norman rulers, who never captured him, though his attacks against them became less frequent. Eventually the Normans assumed he must be dead, although the date of his death, how he died and his place of burial are unknown. Another story tells that he made his peace with William – under what conditions we do not know – and was thereafter treated with honour and respect at the Norman Court. It is also said that in 1072, Wild Edric joined the Norman king in an unsuccessful military expedition into Scotland, after which his fate is not known.

Was his trust in William betrayed, one wonders? Legend suggests that because he made peace and was foolish enough to put his trust in the Normans – being permitted to hold on to his estates, despite William having taken possession of Shropshire as well as all the other counties – Edric and his followers were doomed to a fate worse than death. They were to wander forever in a sleepless afterlife. The old tales narrate how, together with his wife Lady Godda and his supporters, Wild Edric still lives on in the area below Stiperstones, an impressive rocky ridge in the Shropshire Hills, focus for many legends. It was believed to have been a meeting-place for local witch covens and is a recognised walking route still known as Wild Edric's Path; the land beneath is honeycombed with disused lead mines, some going back to Roman times.

It has been suggested that the spirits of Wild Edric and his motley band also occupy some of the actual working mines in Shropshire. By their knocking underground, they are helping the lead miners to locate where the best lodes are situated – in a similar fashion to the weird 'knockers' in the Cornish tin mines.

Edric's story is typical of medieval tales where a human hero gains a fairy bride, and only by breaking some condition she has laid on him might he lose her. Lady Godda forbade that he should ever refer to her fairy origins and he kept his pledge for many years. One day, however, Edric arrived home to find she was not there, and on her return angrily accused her of abandoning him to steal off into the forest to her fairy relatives. At that she disappeared for good and according to yet another story, Edric died of grief. So was it then that he resorted to an eternal after-life in the lead mines?

It is also said that the hero (whether in the lead-mines or not) remains on standby should England become threatened by war. A tall figure dressed in green, riding a white stallion, he has been seen with his phantom army, particularly during times of conflict. He was reported to have appeared in 1853 or 1854, just prior to the Crimean War; he appeared again in 1914, and in September, 1939. And he is still waiting for the next summons.

PART FOUR
GOING HOME

11 'I KNOW WHAT I SAW!'

'I have never believed in any sort of supernatural stuff!'

Dilys and I overheard this declaration at a roadside cafe on the way to Sheffield, where we had stopped for morning coffee only a few weeks ago. The speaker was a prosperous-looking gentleman who was talking to the young woman sharing his table. Being slightly deaf, he spoke rather loudly above the surrounding hubbub, so everyone in the cafe was already aware that it was his eighty-ninth birthday. He also assured his attentive listeners that, as a successful businessman, he had always believed in the concrete, the 'real', the matter-of-fact. He had no truck either with touching wood for luck or any other sort of superstition.

At Psychic and Craft Fairs or other places where I might be appearing and displaying my ghost books, many people tell me the same – sometimes even when they have just related the details of an apparently supernatural happening. Over the years, and after listening to hundreds of such stories, I am no longer amazed how the average person can hold two opposing views at the same time.

As they confide the details of their supernatural experience, they often say they have never told it to anyone before. Words commonly used are: 'I know you'll think this is crazy, but - .' Their story may be recent or have happened many years ago, and always I am impressed by their sincerity as they relive their experience, their efforts to get the details and descriptions right. They try to avoid anomaly and exaggeration, the story when repeated is always exactly the same with no variations. Many say they cannot explain it, they may not believe in the supernatural, but another phrase used in almost every case is - 'I know what I saw!'

I am often asked if I believe in ghosts myself. Personally, I have experienced several ghostly incidents over time and was surprised on each occasion, though never afraid: my curiosity was much stronger. I am also able to 'pick up' on atmospheres. But when I came to write my first book *Living with Ghosts* I was definitely writing more as the 'ghost reporter', an investigator, a fascinated wanderer into the realms of the supernatural. When I needed expert comment I approached people who had had specific experience of working in the various aspects of this extensive field; and of course, I have accompanied Dilys on many occasions when she was carrying out consultations, teaching classes or investigating potential 'hauntings'. I certainly know what I saw and experienced on each of those occasions, but have interviewed Dilys here in order to clarify questions about the nature of psychic vision and the supernatural.

Dilys, what exactly is a psychic person?

Everybody is potentially psychic. What we call 'psychic ability' is a gift, like a gift for music or painting. It just means the person is aware of activity beyond the five senses that we normally use to evaluate our experience – like having an extra sense, a 6th sense. We all have it to some degree but a lot of people don't understand or don't want to use it.

It seems to me that there is a great deal of ignorance about the whole subject. And a kind of mediaeval attitude to the supernatural that has been passed down through the generations. Today's mass media encourages these old fears.

Yes, people often don't really know what they are talking about.

Like the woman who wanted to buy that beautiful Tree of Life pendant from our shop one Christmas, but as soon as you mentioned the Tree of Life had connections with pagan mythology she was horrified and jerked away claiming it was wicked. She obviously didn't realise that the bunch of holly she was carrying was once considered sacred to the Roman God Saturn, and would have been part of the greenery brought indoors at Yuletide, which despite its Christian association, also has its own strong pagan origins. So too, the mistletoe (having been cut from its host, the oak-tree) which was known as the Golden Bough by the Greek pagans, due to its aging berries assuming the colour of gold. This would have connected the winter celebrations with fertility and life-enhancing powers for the year ahead.

A great deal of our everyday living is based on pagan traditions.

I've met people who claim they are very psychic but because of some unpleasant experiences, wish they were not. Does this indicate that there is a form of discipline involved regarding being psychic? You have to learn to deal with it?

The psychic ability, like any other so-called gift, helps you to appreciate life and the world in a fuller way. But many people don't understand their experience, and they aren't aware that there is a far wider concept or picture involved. As with any form of spiritual vision, you do need to work with it to understand any experiences you might have. I might also add that to the gifted person, the gift is as perfectly natural as having an eye for drawing. A lot of so-called 'unpleasant' experiences in this connection happen as a result of ignorant meddling and treating the subject as a game instead of taking it seriously. (There is more on Psychic Protection in Supernatural Snippets No 28).

It is commonly believed that if you are psychic, you just 'see ghosts'. What other things can a psychic do?

The gift isn't intended for you to do things with it or use it in some clever way. Being able to 'see ghosts' is what people think of first, because they don't know of anything else. Again there is a lot of ignorance and superstition here. In fact, by using or working with the gift, the person becomes more spiritually aware and as a result is able to make more sense of life in a wider connection than just the physical or material.

Would you say that someone becomes aware of their psychic abilities early on in life, or might they be unfocused until later – then gradually they become more aware, or due to some sudden event?

All of these can happen. Some people are very aware from babyhood: they might talk about having had spirits around them when very young. Others can undergo a trauma or some kind of life-changing event that makes them become very psychically aware all of a sudden – a lot of women, for example, seem to become 'aware' after having given birth. It might be having undergone a near-death experience, or something dangerous has happened to them.

How did it happen to you?

When I look back I can see that there were indications from when I was a child. You can't become psychic overnight though, so there were years of learning the discipline, which were sometimes very difficult. It's a bit like having a key to unlock a door, but not realising the key is there till something triggers the awareness. Then you have to find the door.

Do you read people's minds?

Yes, but anyone can be a 'sensitive' – the old word for a psychic. The uninformed person thinks that reading the mind is like reading a book, but it doesn't happen like that. I can generally 'see' what someone is thinking, what is in their head. But not specifically, like reading a recipe or a story. Here again, there is a lot of misunderstanding about how the ability works. It would be more accurate to say that you can see the truth, rather than what they are saying, or the impression they want to put out. Some people call a psychic a clairvoyant, the latter meaning 'to see true'. So psychic ability is really seeing the true meaning of things, to whatever degree.

What else do you do?

People often say to me 'What do you do?' because I'm a psychic. The truth is I don't do anything. It's like being able to see in colour when everyone else sees in black and white. You don't have to do anything, it's just there. But what it does give one is a certain amount of power – sometimes a great deal – because others might not have this insight, but anyone who treats the gift as something to exploit for their own ends or gratification has got the wrong idea altogether. If it is abused like that, then either it is withdrawn, blocked, or you find that such people are taught a lesson and have to approach it again in the right way. The gift does not belong to you – it is lent in a very spiritual sense.

But I know you use the Tarot cards. What about using crystals – and a crystal ball? Or the runes?

I use the cards as a focus for the clairvoyant vision, the 'Sight' or whatever you want to call it. The crystal ball and the runes are also to some degree triggers to focus the psychic ability, and there are similar disciplines that work the same way. Psychometry – holding an object – for instance, allows the psychic to 'tune in' to atmospheres or vibrations that give him or her insight about the owner of the object. A crystal ball is another focus, but it only allows psychic insight, it does not actually 'tell fortunes'. Nobody can 'tell fortunes' as such, only perhaps be able to predict potential happenings or trends. Crystals themselves possess individual energies that can empower or heal in different ways. The runes are a system of connecting with the power of the natural world or the universe by means of sounds, sometimes by the name of the rune itself when written down. The runes are more about knowing when the time is right, going with the flow.

What about reading people's palms? Or astrology?

Both palmistry and astrology are separate disciplines with their own rules and guidelines. You don't have to be psychic to work as a palmist or an astrologer. If you learn what the lines on the hand mean or the positions of the planets (rather than the stars) and the rules of astrology, you will probably find you can be successful without any real psychic awareness.

When you have been working in a room with other psychics, I've noticed that you rarely do readings (whether with the Tarot cards, palmistry or whatever method) for young people. The ones who are interested only in job and marriage prospects seem to go to someone else. So is this deliberate? Do you prefer to do consultations for more mature people?

There are a lot of assumptions in that question. But if you regard a child or young person as similar to a growing plant or flower, it is very difficult from my point of view to say anything helpful. The person's potential far outweighs any definite development of personality – you could say that it's trying to comment on the beauty of a flower when it hasn't even yet formed a bud. Children and young people are still so influenced by those around them, they have not yet formed a character of their own. A discipline like astrology would be more helpful in their case – a bit more scientific.

I personally find I can't be helpful with surface queries about going to Uni, or meeting a potential partner. My work is concerned with people who are more 'on their way' spiritually – the progress of their soul. I am more likely to work at a different level. And young people are still being taught by their teachers. You can't go trespassing. With older people in their mid-twenties, thirties etc., if they have not moved on, then something has blocked them. They can be helped to 'flower' as it were. This is different to simply 'reading the cards'. It is seeing the appropriateness of everything, helping them see the truth about themselves and for me to see the truth about myself, too.

My feeling is that psychics like Dilys obviously 'see' or experience things and happenings that are, in a physical sense, utterly impossible. Yet obviously they too 'know what they see!'

*

There is a legend that if you ran round the outside of the Church of St Nicholas at Canewdon, in Essex, on the 31st of October, you would travel through time. 'Time-slips' are occasions where someone is conscious of finding themselves, even if for just a few moments – or seconds – in a different age to the one they are normally part of.

The writer Joan Foreman included such instances in her book *The Mask of Time* – one case was that of an elderly man she referred to as Mr Squirrel. A keen coin-collector from Norfolk in the 1970s, he travelled to Great Yarmouth to a stationer's shop, in order to purchase some small transparent envelopes in which to store his coins. Although he had never been there before, the establishment had been recommended and he had been told the way.

On arriving he noticed that the street was cobble-stoned and entering the shop, which was dark and completely silent, he saw an old-fashioned, box-like till. On sale were walking-sticks, photo-frames and various *bric a brac*. The young woman who came to his assistance wore a long black skirt, blouse with 'mutton-chop' sleeves and her hair was piled on top of her head. She was able to supply him with the small transparent envelopes he had requested, charging him one shilling. Without thinking (decimal coinage having been introduced in 1973) he automatically offered her a new 5 pence coin, the equivalent of an old shilling piece. She stared at it without comment before accepting it and he left the shop thinking little more about the experience – until he returned to the shop shortly afterwards for a further supply of envelopes.

As he turned the corner into the street, he saw with some surprise that it was no longer cobble-stoned but covered by modern (and weathered!) paving-slabs. The shop itself was there, but he was served by an older woman who knew nothing of the young assistant he had encountered on his previous visit. She informed Mr Squirrel that the establishment had none of the transparent envelopes he wanted, and had never stocked them.

So had all this been some sort of hallucination? Joan Foreman carried out further research and was able to trace the makers of the small transparent envelopes in question. She discovered they had in fact been on sale during the 1920s; and had even been manufactured prior to 1914. What added interest to the case was that Mr Squirrel actually still had in his possession some of the envelopes he had purchased from the early 20th century stationer's shop.

Obviously he had 'gone back' in time without realising it and had dealings with a ghost from the past. But 'time-slips' can be subtler than more usual 'hauntings'; in cases like this, it sometimes happens that the person in the 'time-slip', like the young assistant in the shop, have also reported their experience, thinking they too were seeing a ghost – but in their case, a ghost from the future.

'Time-slips' may be far more common than we realise, regarded as strange, but not as 'seeing ghosts'. And though the person concerned might not be able to explain what happened, he will remember very well 'what he saw!'

On 3rd October 1963, at 9 am, Coleen Buterbaugh, a secretary at Nebraska Wesleyan University in Lincoln, Nebraska, was asked by the Dean Sam Dahl to deliver a message to Professor Martin, who had offices in the C.C. White Building nearby. Once there Mrs Buterbaugh pushed through the throng of chattering music students in the hall, who were making their way to their various classes. From one of the rooms used for rehearsals, she distinctly heard someone playing the marimba.

As she entered Professor Martin's offices, she felt overcome by an unfamiliar, powerful odour which almost made her choke. She also had the feeling that she was not alone; and realized everywhere had become deadly silent, including the hallway behind her where she had just encountered the students. Coleen caught the back view of a woman in the adjoining room, who was reaching up to a set of shelves in a cabinet against the wall. Her figure was poised, perfectly still as though she was part of a waxworks. Coleen later described her as tall, her black hair bouffant, and wearing a blouse and long skirt. She felt instinctively that the woman was not real – then the figure vanished.

Coleen then glanced through the office window and saw a group of trees in an open field. She could not make out why neither the building connected to the University, with which she was familiar, nor the busy street outside, appeared to be there! Frightened, she backed out into the hallway to find the students still chattering on their way to classes, and the marimba still being played.

She realised that what she had just experienced must have lasted only a few seconds, and that the figure she encountered had not been of her time. She told Dean Dahl that she herself had gone back to the era of the strange woman, since she had seen trees and open space through the window. From the records, a photograph was eventually found (which Coleen Buterbaugh had not previously seen) of a former lecturer, Miss Clarissa Mills, who had arrived at the establishment in 1912. Her mode of dress and hairstyle, as described by Coleen, would have fitted the fashions of that time. Her death came suddenly in 1936, after she had struggled through inclement weather one morning, on her way to the University.

Miss Mills had also been involved in choral singing, and the cabinet where her apparition had appeared contained a number of scores, predating her death. Professor Martin, a visiting professor from Scotland (the person to whom Coleen Bauterbaugh had been asked to deliver a message from Dean Dahl) was, at the time, involved in making arrangements of some of those actual scores for the choral class.

So did the spirit of Miss Mills still feel involved in the project? Or had her death occurred so suddenly that she did not realize she had left her place of work?

Any one of us might find ourselves caught up in such a time-slip without realising the fact. Our friend Helen told me the story of Mike, who a few years ago, lived in a second-floor bedsit in Buxton. Hurrying down the stairs one day, he had the vague impression that the wallpaper had changed from something plain to a bold flowery design; on the ground-floor, through an open door, he saw a man and a woman in the room with a child, all dressed in Victorian/Edwardian clothing.

His mind elsewhere, Mike thought nothing of it at the time, since there were normally all sorts of events staged in the nearby Pavilion Gardens for the sake of tourists who visited the town. It

157

was some time later that the landlord, who knew he was a painter and decorator by profession, asked him to repaper and repaint the stairs and hallway, which Mike agreed to undertake. But when he came to scrape off the plain wallpaper, it was with acute surprise that he found revealed underneath, the bold, flowery-designed wallpaper he had fleetingly encountered not long before.

Dilys and I experienced a possible 'time-slip' a short time after our encounter with the mysterious Ford Transit van described earlier – and on the same stretch of road. We came up the narrow, winding B6049 late one night, having passed through Millers Dale, to join the main road to Buxton. Above the trees that closed in on the road, we saw a number of searchlights criss-crossing as they scanned the dark sky. They appeared to originate in the town, yet as we drove nearer, the source of the lights seemed to recede into the distance towards Stoke-on-Trent, some twenty miles away.

Like the strange sounds described in Supernatural Snippets No 24, 'always somewhere else when the observer moves to the locality from which they first seemed to come', the lights filled the sky ahead but seemed to have no identifiable place where they originated. We made enquiries later – thinking there might have been some sort of public display taking place – but could find no answer, although one other person admitted to having seen the searchlights herself. I think what we had seen were searchlights within a time-slip from the 1940s – during the Second World War.

Whether we believe in the supernatural or not, it is likely that every one of us will have some sort of paranormal experience (perhaps more than one) to a greater or lesser degree during our lifetime. Some of us may have experienced the paranormal already without realising the full significance of what has happened. Not all ghosts appear as outlandish or frightening and while there are people who do 'see ghosts' all their lives, others may not see ghosts as such but be very 'clairsentient', aware of presences. There are many different way of using the psychic gift and a clairsentient person is not necessarily more or less advanced than someone who witnesses a ghostly presence with their own two eyes.

Dilys says that as a psychic medium, she 'sees' ghosts, or spirits by way of her 'mind's eye', by entering another dimension. I have experienced something similar on only one occasion, but have viewed many other ghosts using my normal eyesight. And again, like most people who have such stories to tell, I know what I saw!

12 ACROSS THE THRESHOLD

We all recognise that death, like birth, is a major happening. As to what happens afterwards, despite the teachings of various faiths, the fact is we do not know. We can only surmise. The philosopher Bertrand Russell believed that the only thing after death was 'rot', referring to the decay, or breakdown of the physical body, discarded like a pair of old overalls. That is the one fact we do know of.

It has been suggested that a spirit experiencing severe shock by suddenly being wrenched from the physical body by way of a heart-attack, road accident or in battle, will need to overcome the trauma by means of rest and possibly some kind of recuperative treatment. We have no real evidence about what happens to the departed spirit or soul once it has crossed from life to death, though there are endless suppositions – and superstitions.

At dusk, a spectral hound is sometimes seen padding its way along a road by Bartholmey Rectory, in Cheshire, its appearance believed to be an omen of death. In coastal areas, it was once assumed you could not die unless the tide was going out. If the dying man did survive an ebb tide, he was bound to linger until the next. Another belief once respected being that it was more natural to die in contact with the earth from which all men originated, is thought to have spawned from times when most cottages had floors of earth. A dying person was usually lifted from his bed and laid on the cold earth floor to accelerate his demise in a proper – but thoughtful – manner.

In Cumberland and counties further north, a particular vigil used to be held every 24th April, the Eve of the Feast of St Mark. The Rev W. Close once wrote that: 'In olden days it was a common belief that if you went into your churchyard between 11 pm and 1 am on St Mark's Eve, you would see pass before you the spirits of friends and neighbours who would die before St Mark's Day a year hence. It was a morbid watch, but one generally adopted.' A Mr Brocket, who wrote about old Northumberland customs, stated in 1829 that spirits of those who were to die within a year of each St Mark's Eve would pass through their parish churchyard wearing their usual day clothes.

Corpse Lights were once considered dire warnings of death. Resulting from ignited marsh gas, they would float over ground between a churchyard and the home of the person about to leave this world, indicating the route that the funeral procession would ultimately take. According to folklore, again in Cumberland, a 'death light' was often seen as the spirit left the body. Old people still relate how their grandparents told them of such lights also seen when they had visited houses where a death had recently occurred. If it concerned the death of a child, the flame would be blue; if yellow, it would have marked the passing of an adult.

In many parts of the country various customs were once observed concerning people who had only recently died. One was to cover up all mirrors in the house, or turn them to the wall, where the deceased lay because it was believed that for a period, the spirit of the corpse would stay around. It was considered unlucky for those in the household should the spirit catch a glimpse of itself in the glass. Doors and windows would be opened and all animals and pets were put out of doors until after the funeral, to prevent the passing spirit from entering through them. The domestic fire would sometimes be allowed to go out. After all, it represented the life of the household. Clocks, too, would be stopped – the dead no longer being concerned about time.

During the 18th century someone paying his last respects in the house of the deceased person might well have been asked to become a 'sin-eater' by consuming food and drink over the corpse, and accepting a small gift of money. By so doing, he would take on the responsibility of the dead person's sins. Visitors would touch the brow of the corpse out of respect, so preventing themselves from being troubled by the dead man's ghost. It was also believed that the body of someone who had been murdered would bleed if touched by his killer. Other visitors who paid their respects might actually have touched the flesh of the corpse, prior to touching their own. Should the touch prove to feel cold to their own skin, they would be dismayed, in the belief that they themselves would be dead within the year.

In Germany, and many other countries, it is believed that anyone who lies in a coffin as some sort of game is inviting their own death. Clothing belonging to a living person should never be used as a shroud for the corpse when put into the coffin. Otherwise once in the grave, as the clothing rots, so the health of the living owner will sink into serious decline and eventual death.

To show further respect for the deceased, the coffin would have been kept company by a vigil of family, friends and neighbours. A corpse, it was believed, should never be left on its own between its death and the funeral, nor locked in an empty house, particularly at night. If this happened, it would have been considered shocking and neglectful of a prime duty.

Following the funeral, the Wake, particularly in later years, would have been a sombre ritual, with readings from the Bible, amid hushed, reverential voices. In earlier times, the Wake was a livelier affair with lots of merry-making, singing, dancing, playing card-games and indulging in practical jokes. The occasion was considered no less disrespectful to the deceased, for it was assumed that such revelry helped protect him, or her, on the long journey that lay ahead, besides offering comfort to the bereaved relatives. Of pagan origin, sometimes candles to provide light, and food for sustenance were placed in the coffin, to help further the anticipated journey, with a hammer to knock on the door of the ultimate destination. Later, a copy of the Bible and a certificate from Sunday-school would have been included, to vouch for the

163

devoutness of the person concerned. Quite often in Victorian times, toys were interred with children who had died, and some cherished object to give equal comfort would be placed in the coffin of a deceased adult. This would have originated from the old pagan belief that such objects would be needed in the Next World as much as they were useful in that of our own.

In the West, black has been the official colour of mourning since Roman times, when it also bore associations with the Underworld. During the 19th century, the Victorians would have displayed their state of mourning for about a year following the death of a family member. The widow's veil, together with other sombre clothing was assumed to prevent their being recognised by any angry ghosts that might have been around. At a child's funeral, it was customary for a bearer, wearing a white sash and, carrying a white standard, to precede the white coffin. Any innocent girl who died before marriage was usually commemorated with a Maiden's Garland, with white gloves pinned to it, and which, after the funeral, would have been hung in the church.

The burial garment was usually a shroud. Some were made ready long before they were needed. In the north-east of England, girls would include them, as a matter of course, in their trousseaux. In the event of a bride dying soon after marriage she would normally have been buried in her wedding dress. Sometimes, the deceased were buried in their own clothes, while those in the armed forces were often laid to rest in their uniforms, while gypsies were 'seen away' wearing their very best clothes. People in holy orders, like nuns and monks were interred in their habits.

In 1962, it was reported that the ghostly figure of a monk with a pronounced limp had been seen for many years crossing the garden of a house in Cathedral Close, in Winchester. It would then pass through a wall before going into the Cathedral and disappearing. When the wall was eventually pulled down three skeletons were discovered near its foundations. It was thought they had, for some reason, been buried in haste and that the victims had once belonged to a medieval monastic order. The leg-bones of one showed distinct signs of arthritis which would have caused the monk concerned considerable pain and to have walked with a pronounced limp. Once the skeletons had been reburied, with appropriate ceremony, the ailing monk has never been seen since.

A story tells of Joseph Wilson who once haunted Brigham churchyard, where his remains were interred in 1757. As the local hangman he was said to have been sorely troubled by the number of people he had 'seen off'. In a misguided effort to find peace, he threw himself off Cocker Bridge, at Cockermouth. Over a century later, a gravedigger, while working in Brigham churchyard, discovered the hangman's skull; carefully placing it in a box he took it to Wilson's old home. Put into a cupboard, it remained there for some years, all trace of it eventually being lost. Whether or not a reburial took place, Joseph Wilson no longer haunted Brigham churchyard. Perhaps the spirit of the troubled hangman had found much-sought peace at last.

Fulford House in Dunsford, Devon, was once haunted by the local squire who had been buried 'not proper to his wishes'. A parson advised that to enable Squire Fulford to attain everlasting peace, the villagers should dig up his corpse and, on reburying it on the bank of the local river, they should bind and tie it down firmly. This they supposedly did, yet his ghost appeared again soon afterwards, walking but one cock-stride nearer to Fulford House, each night, witnesses believing it would take a great deal of time to attain its goal. However, it was soon suspected that the parson's advice had been ignored and that the body of Squire Fulford remained where he had been buried in the first place. Attracting him to his familiar surroundings like Fulford House was the possibility that some of his personal belongings still remained there.

Angela Cutting, author of *Leicestershire Ghost Stories*, tells us of when her grandparents moved into a house along Brandon Street in Leicester, shortly after the previous owner of the property, an elderly woman, had died; her daughter being their immediate neighbour. One night when the elderly couple had gone to bed, they heard movement downstairs. At first, they thought burglars had gained entry. Then they were aware of footsteps coming up the stairs. Their bedroom door opened suddenly and the figure of an elderly woman entered. Aghast, the couple recognised her as the previous owner, whom they had known quite well when she was alive. Approaching the bed, she stared at them for a moment then left, her footsteps heard retreating back down the stairs.

Next morning, the couple were informed that the daughter of their night-time visitor had been found dead in the garden, next door. Although shaken by their experience, they concluded that their deceased friend must have briefly returned in order to take her daughter 'home'.

There was also the strange case of a Polish saint. Most citizens of Prague know that their historic Charles Bridge, which spans the Vlatava River, is haunted. During the Middle Ages, the severed heads of several noblemen were displayed there on pikes. Their mournful cries, so it is said, can still be heard by anyone who crosses the bridge at the stroke of midnight.

An equally sinister touch is the presence of thirty or so Gothic statues that line the bridge. One of them, however, represents St John of Nepomuk, a Cistercian priest who in 1393 was summoned to the Castle by King Wenceslas IV, who demanded to know everything about a confession the priest had recently taken with his wife, Queen Johanna. John refused, telling the king that what passed between a priest and a member of his flock concerned no-one except themselves – and God. Enraged, the king immediately ordered the priest to be tortured, and thrown from the bridge into the river below. For more than 300 years, John's ghost was seen either on the bridge itself or wandering along the river bank.

It was during the 17th century that the statue was placed on the bridge, in his name. Anyone who touches the statue of St John, and wishes to disclose any secrets they may have, may feel rest assured that those secrets will remain as such in his hands. Perhaps St John of Nepomuk, in his own way, now feels he has achieved his own manner of 'going home'.

First reported in 1795 by the Rev. Dr James Clegg, a Nonconformist minister of Chapel-en-le-Frith, was when, before a number of eye-witnesses, several hundred bodies rose from a flood victims' mass grave in the cemetery of the Old Chapel at Hayfield, in Derbyshire. Singing together, they ascended directly towards Heaven, naked but not appearing to be so. Their ascent was swift, according to the Reverend Doctor, their leaving a wonderfully fragrant scent after them. Had they really 'gone home' in so public a manner? Opinion has it that he had probably invented the story in order to emphasise the Resurrection of the Body. It could also be a more theatrical account of what happens when, put into a shallow, hastily prepared mass grave, the bodies of flood victims, bloated with water, may return to the surface of the ground. The idea has tended to create a considerable amount of folklore in Europe and many other parts of the world. Although, of course, bodies in that condition would only rise to the surface if they had been lying in a mass grave which itself was flooded.

Hugh Robertson Black, a long-standing friend of ours, witnessed an equally interesting incident a few years ago. His job in Holmfirth involved making a journey from Cheadle, Stoke-on-Trent, via the Peak District and joining the main Manchester to Sheffield Road (A628).

Before going further over the moors to his final destination, he regularly stopped off at Crowden, taking a pot-holed climb off the main road in the car to have a picnic, seated on the steps of the local chapel. There he would sit surrounded by a cemetery – and on a summer's day, with an incredible view across the peaceful valley, despite the traffic on the road, far below. He told me that on one occasion, he became aware of bodies rising from the surrounding graves at an angle of 45 degrees; not so much solid, but more like pale forms, almost transparent.

'I simply turned my head sideways and said silently: "Not yet! Get back down!" And, to my surprise, they had done so when I looked again!' Hugh reported, adding that he wasn't at all frightened at the time, feeling reassured by the fine summer's day remaining as before.

Breaking his journey, Hugh would have felt relaxed, having arrived at such a beautiful area – panoramic and expansive enough for the endless landscape to meld with the sun and the varying blues of the sky. It can be at such times that one might suddenly become attuned, however briefly, to that alternative dimension – a timeless universe, if you like – something totally unplanned. I have seen a number of drawings illustrating the spirit leaving the body at the moment of death, interestingly at an angle of 45 degrees. At a location such as a cemetery, we might assume that the spirits would have long left the bodies that have lain there for various lengths of time. So what Hugh witnessed, who knows? Were these bodies collectively mistaking the glorious day for that of the Day of Judgement? Only to be directed by Hugh that it was not yet time to rise.

Renowned for his interest in Celtic mysticism, the ghosts of Roman Britain and the passing of the centuries, was the British composer John Ireland. During the 1930s, he was based in Ashington, on the Downs and was keenly aware of the Neolithic associations of the area, which had once included a leper colony.

One day while out walking, he sat down in the sun in a similar manner to Hugh, to enjoy his packed lunch – only to be confronted by several children, dancing. This annoyed the composer at first – before he realised that they were dressed in old-fashioned clothes and were playing in complete silence. For a second, he looked away and to his surprise, they suddenly vanished. He wrote to his friend, the mystical writer, Arthur Machen, about the incident. 'So you've seen them too!' was the reply he later received by postcard. Unable to identify the ghostly children, the experience affected John Ireland profoundly and is thought to have triggered the idea for his atmospheric composition *Legend for Piano and Orchestra*, first performed in January, 1934.

An atmospheric story surrounds a young woman who died of a broken heart being interred in Warden Churchyard, Northumberland – date not given. Afterwards, 'a singular and uncommon species of yellow flower, similar to that of mustard' established itself on her grave. At the end of the season, however, it disappeared, never to flower again. An appearance, and ultimate disappearance, of an unknown flower on a grave was significant in folklore concerning death by means of a broken heart.

There is also a belief reflected in some old ballads such as *Lord Lovel* and *The Lass of Loch Royal* that such unfamiliar flowers often appear on the graves of star-crossed lovers. The fact that their stems intertwine, even forming a lovers' knot, indicates that love never ends, even in death. There is also a hint that the soul of the dead lover is represented by the plant. For the young woman buried in Wardle Churchyard it could have stood for her short life, her having flowered briefly, before moving on.

What might the presence of trees signify in a churchyard? An extremely obese man named Ben Wangford, who lived in Watford, Hertfordshire in the mid 18th century, held no belief whatsoever in the Hereafter. Following his death, he had left instructions for 'something to be placed' in his grave. If it grew his family would know that his spirit was still alive. If it didn't, it would show that his opinion about the Hereafter had been justified. Eventually, a fine fig tree emerged and was the talk of the town. In fact, 'The Fig Tree Tomb, Watford' as it became known as, was a mecca for tourists over many years, the tree surviving, until it fell victim to the harsh winter of 1962-63.

Something similar concerned Lady Anne Grimston who, aged sixty, died on 22nd November, 1713. The wife of Sir Samuel Grimston, Baronet of Gorhambury, she was buried in St Peter's Churchyard at Tewin, also in Hertfordshire, her tomb surrounded by iron railings. As with Ben Wangford, there was some debate regarding her religious beliefs as to whether God existed or not. On her death-bed she pronounced that if He *did* exist then seven ash-trees would grow against her tombstone – which they did.

SUPERNATURAL SNIPPETS No 4
Going Home

23 - Celestial Music

As in previous times of conflict, World War Two saw everyone in a shared state of heightened awareness, when realities could easily expand into altered states of consciousness. But Basil Saville, a former choir-boy at St Alban's Abbey in Hertfordshire, did not believe in the supernatural. On Christmas Eve, 1944, he was the first to arrive at the large Norman abbey as part of a fire-watching team, whose job it was to keep vigilance all night in case of fire-bombs being dropped by enemy planes. His only source of light was a regulation hooded torch, though outside there was a full moon – 'a Bombers' Moon'. Basil knew the building well, but checking the water containers, stirrup-pumps and hoses, he had an uneasy sense that he was being watched – that he was not alone in the building, despite the fact that none of his fellow fire-watchers had yet arrived.

Shining his torch towards an upper level, he thought he caught sight of two hooded figures and shouted a challenge, then swiftly mounted the stairs to discover two monks' habits lying on the floor. He had no idea where they had come from. Then as he was checking the area above the nave, a bell began to toll; he became even more concerned because, for safety reasons, the bells were being stored for the duration of hostilities on the ground floor. As he approached the belfry the tolling stopped and Basil could see for himself that no bell remained there. By now he was becoming alarmed. Making his way down from the belfry, he heard the organ start to play while a candle flickered near to the console, the light so dim he was unable to see who was playing.

Basil shouted 'Put that light out!' and moved closer. To his consternation the music grew louder, the individual keys of the organ seeming to be manipulated by unseen fingers, while the pages of the score were being turned by some invisible hand. From the high altar then came a burst of glorious choral singing. Hardly knowing what to do, Basil made his way through the abbey and down to the choir stalls – at which the music stopped. Gazing at the high altar, he turned to see a procession of monks led by an abbot, each holding a lighted candle, leave through the doors leading to the Saints Chapel. Swiftly following them, he found the place dank, dark – and deserted.

Investigating the organ loft again by the light of his hooded torch, he found the spent candle and a music-score where the notes were written on very old manuscript paper, protected between two thick covers labelled the *Albanus Mass* by Robert Fayrfax – the original score which had been discovered in the abbey some years before, Fairfax having been Master of the King's Musick to Henry VIII early in the 16th century, as well as organist and director of the choir of St Alban's Abbey.

By now Basil Saville was very shaken. He thought he heard something moving around in the vestry and to his relief, this turned out to be the arrival of a fellow fire-watcher, to whom he described what had just happened. Both men went to the organ loft, where they saw no sign of any candle or manuscript; neither did they find the two monks' habits Basil had seen earlier. It emerged later that for a long time there had been stories of a phantom organist in St Alban's Abbey, playing during the late hours of darkness. There were also accounts of Benedictine monks appearing and disappearing through the walls and closed doors of the great ecclesiastical edifice.

A place of similar interest is the former Avenbury Church near Bromyard, in Herefordshire, now in ruins. It is believed that the organist there was murdered by his brother and in spite of the site being exorcised, ghostly organ music is still said to emanate from the deserted location. Adding to the mystery is the tale that one of the original bells, now installed in St Andrew-by-the-Wardrobe in London, tolls whenever an Avenbury vicar dies.

24 - Strange Sounds

Arguably, today our lives are filled with noise to the point of overkill – from blazingly loud car radios, television, roaring planes, and everyday town and city traffic, to pulsating music downloads. For only brief intervals might we experience complete silence – or even pick up on those strange, unaccountable sounds that can hint at supernatural activity. These we may hear in a quieter location, in the same way our forefathers encountered them in less hectic times.

Strange, but soothing airborne sounds were heard in 1890 by Edwin Linton, a scientist connected to the U.S. Fish Commission, when working at Yellowstone Lake, in Wyoming. He and a colleague described them as echoes, with slightly metallic reverberations. They seemed to begin overhead, move south-west, each of about 30 seconds' duration. Occasionally they sounded like wind, yet the lake and surrounding trees appeared perfectly calm. Other people heard them two years later and they were also reported in 1919. The phenomenon was duly entered in the *Ranger Naturalists' Manual* but was never explained.

Booming sounds – but unrelated to thunder or earthquakes – were known to fishermen in the North Sea for many years. Heard when conditions were quiet but misty, the fishermen referred to them as *mist-poeffers*; while in the Indian Ganges Delta, similar phenomena were known as the Barisal guns. It was in 1934 that

Albert G. Ingalls, familiar with what were now described as the 'guns of Seneca Lake' in upstate New York, described them in *Science* magazine. 'Their direction is vague,' he wrote, 'and like the foot of a rainbow, they are always somewhere else when the observer moves to the locality from which they first seemed to come.'

When settlers first established themselves in the Connecticut River valley – where the towns of Moodus and East Haddam were built – they were informed by the troubled native Indians that the unearthly sounds were of their own gods showing anger at the 'imported' English god. Here the sounds were connected to earth tremors, but, strangely, not any tremors at Moodus, although we might wonder if the 'earthly disturbances' actually caused, or were the result, of the atmospheric occurrences.

Serious attempts to explain the strange phenomena began towards the end of the 19th century, when Ernest Van den Broeck from Belgium collected a mass of testimonies concerning the *mist-poeffers* from the Bay of Biscay, right up to Iceland. Many theories were published in various scientific journals. Van den Broeck suggested the causes were due to 'some peculiar kind of discharge of atmospheric electricity' (i.e. thunder – but from clear blue skies?). It was also said that the mysterious bangs originated from the activity of liquid rock (magma) at the centre of the earth. Other theories hinted such sounds were associated with coastal areas and river deltas, whereby accumulated sediment caused the earth beneath to settle on a grand scale. However, this would have caused tidal waves which had not been experienced.

The splitting of boulders due to subterranean stresses, too, was put forward. But where this takes place beneath the sea, a high-pitched sound is produced rather than loud bangs. One Father Saderra Maso, who had studied meteorology in the Philippines, was sure that the bangs were in some way connected to waves breaking on shores and in caves, prior to approaching typhoons.

He also suggested that certain atmospheric conditions (not specified) were responsible for the long distances that such sounds could travel – could their origins have been inland, reflected off cumulus clouds in mountainous regions?

None of these vague theories stand up to scientific scrutiny, however. The ancient gods can still play a trick or two – and some answers are meant to remain a mystery.

25 - Tradition Lingers

One could say that a haunted place, or one with a particular atmosphere, might have been 'stained' by some incident – whether an act of violence or one of feelings, positive or negative having persisted as a result of the people who once lived there, passed through the vicinity on a regular basis, or even just one dramatic occasion. The 'stain' may take time to heal – in some cases, a *very* long time, maybe with the original incident being repeated over centuries before the supernatural power finally dissolves or, like a battery, seemingly runs low, any ghosts having eventually gone their way with or without the help of a psychic.

We can all recall places such as a derelict old house on the edge of a lonely wood, isolated rocks or trees, pools or river crossings, anywhere we remember where for no real reason we were uncomfortable; our 'collective unconscious' persuading us that the place must have been haunted - by ghosts or by something. In truth, it might never have been haunted, except by the rumours.

The collective unconscious works in a mysterious way within what we know and accept as fact. For instance, in the Spitfire Gallery at the Potteries Museum and Art Gallery in Stoke-on-Trent, some visitors have been aware of powerful energies they believed emanated from the plane on show, representing the acrid smell of battle, smoke and burning oil. But the fact is that the particular plane on display here never saw active service. So does the simple viewing of the Spitfire – despite it having long been superseded by more sophisticated successors – still conjure up the horrific atmosphere of desperate endeavour and war in the air, even though the facts do not back this up?

Arguably, such folklore is based on an awareness rightly or wrongly implanted in the collective unconscious; people recall such awareness over time, like far off memories persisting, their origins not easy to recall. Some ghostly stories may seem highly improbable. Some may become distorted by repetition, plausible explanations emerging or not, as the case may be. There might be no reason for long-standing traditions; when investigation is carried out the whole tale may prove to have no foundation: as a journalist, Dilys once undertook to write an article about a glittering underground banquet lit by thousands of candles, supposedly held for the Tsar of Russia when he visited the salt mines in Cheshire. When she began to research the story however, she discovered that no Tsar of Russia had ever visited the salt mines, let alone attended an underground banquet in his honour. As officials at the mines today pointed out, it would have been completely impossible to hold an event such as was described in such a location. So where did the story – well known in local tradition – originate?

On the other hand, unsuspected truths may emerge from the complexities of local folklore. The Normans once referred to a particular site as the 'Lake of Blood', situated in East Sussex. This was where the Battle of Hastings was fought in 1066. It is claimed that the ground to this day still oozes blood whenever it rains – though more realistically, it is the iron present in the soil that is thought to be responsible for the fact that any puddles forming during wet weather appear to be tinted with red.

There are various explanations for a ghost story that concerns the grossly unpopular King John, whose name is a byword for historical villainy (especially regarding the stories of Robin Hood).

Despite signing Magna Carta, the cornerstone of English Law in 1215, it is said that he was so wicked that after his death he haunted Surrey in the form of a werewolf. There have indeed been reports in recent years of a large animal – 'the Surrey Puma' - running wild in the area, which tradition inevitably tries to link with the infamous Royal individual.

Heydon Ditch, an ancient earthwork in Cambridgeshire, runs for a distance of three-and-a-half miles between Heydon and Fowlmere. Mysterious ghostly warriors of enormous height were seen over the years wandering around the ditch and in the surrounding fields; no-one really knew anything of the earthworks' history, but it was vaguely assumed that it had been built by the Saxons as a defence against the British. Perhaps prompted by such sightings, archaeological investigations were carried out in the 1950s – to reveal the burial pits of a number of headless skeletons of tall Saxon soldiers.

Similarly, an area of unenclosed land known as Heaven's Wall, close to the Roman road at Litlington (also in Cambridgeshire), was traditionally believed to be haunted, though no actual sightings were reported so no-one knew who or what it was haunted by. At the beginning of the 19th century, by chance while digging for gravel, some workmen unearthed a wall of flint and Roman brick. Later digging carried out by experts revealed an enclosed area in which there were a number of funerary urns containing human ashes. This type of Roman cemetery is called an *ustrinum*, for the burial of ashes of the ordinary dead, with the minimum ceremony and expense; in his 1908 book *Folklore as an Historical Science*, the author G.L. Gomme provided a plan of the site, including a nearby Roman tomb and the foundations of a Roman villa, all long forgotten except by local folk-memory.

26 - Animal Power

It may seem strange today that our distant ancestors saw little difference between animals and themselves. They even thought it possible to assume non-human forms and adopt animals as mates. As recently as the late 19th century Baubi Urquhart, a woman from Shetland, declared that the wife of her great-great-grandfather had been a seal. Indeed, legends arose out of the belief that the human spirit was able to live on in certain animals. Seals were thought to represent Pharoah's armies drowned in the Red Sea as they pursued the Children of Israel; while the spirits of drowned sailors were said to be transformed into seagulls.

In Celtic belief many animals and birds have always been looked upon either as 'lucky' or 'unlucky' oracles with regard to individual human destinies. Some beliefs, in a rich mixture of paganism and Christianity, are reflected to this day. In Somerset, by carrying an onion, you are protected against the fear and sorrow the sight of a single magpie may have upon you. In Scotland it was once regarded as so evil a bird because it was thought to carry a drop of the Devil's blood hidden beneath its tongue. You might even have spat three times over your right shoulder and once at the creature, calling: 'Devil, I defy thee!' After all, it is rumoured that one of the sins committed by the magpie was that it failed to wear full mourning at the time of the Crucifixion.

Foxes too, were once associated with the Devil, and a bite from the animal was considered to be fatal. A bite from a pig was believed to cause cancer; while eating pigs' brains caused people to speak the truth. By contrast, it is said that at midnight on Christmas Eve, sheep will face the east to respect the birth of Jesus Christ. Because these animals possessed healing powers, children were often placed where sheep had lain in order to cure them of whooping cough. The hare was once regarded as sacred, but by the Middle Ages had unwittingly become associated with witchcraft.

According to wide belief at the time, witches were able to transform themselves into hares.

Ancient British mythology regarded a number of animals as sacred, including cats, dogs, snakes, pigs and cows – all thought to possess psychic powers. Dogs and horses are said to be able to see ghosts, but while dogs may snarl and tremble at something unseen by the human eye, the horse will sweat and shy. It was the clairvoyant abilities of the horse which made it possible for the souls of the Celts to journey on its back to the territory of the dead. Even so, the horse was still vulnerable to the powers of the Evil Eye. That was the reason why – in more recent times – horse-owners protected them with decorative horse-brasses, often in the spirit-repelling shapes of the crescent moon and the sun.

A bird thought to be a harbinger of bad luck was the owl, known to Pliny, the Roman historian who, in 77 AD, described the Screech Owl as ' the most execrable and accursed'! Swallows nesting under the eaves of a building each year are said to protect the structure from storms and lightning. If a swallow happened to fly into the house, it brought with it only joy. Killing a swallow or destroying its nest, meant that a member of the household would die also, or the house would go up in flames as a consequence.

The robin's red breast originated, according to folklore, when the bird was singed when it took pity and delivered water to sinners burning in Hell. An alternative version suggests that the robin was splashed with the blood of Christ as He suffered on the Cross.

In Shropshire, it is said that the plaintive calls of curlews, or plovers signify they are looking for a mate that has gone missing for good – or so it would seem. Their eventually finding it, however, would mean the end of the world. Such plaintive calls, according to folklore, may alternatively represent the deeply-distressed spirits of un-baptised children condemned to roam the heavens forever.

The dove, on the other hand, has come to stand for purity, peace and reconciliation – and it is an important Christian symbol. Thus, witches who claimed they could change themselves into almost any animal they chose were unable to change into a dove. And as long as any patient lay on a mattress stuffed with dove feathers, it was believed he would soon recover. But surprisingly, they could also be omens of death; if doves flew round someone's head or settled on the roof of their dwelling, the spirit would quietly leave the body of that person and go comfortably and peacefully on its way.

27 - Out of Body

What is an out-of-body experience (an OOBE)? Many people have claimed to experience visions of the departed, but seeing someone who is not physically present need not necessarily mean they have died. An example of an OOBE is when someone's spirit has apparently left their (still living) body and is seen elsewhere – maybe even appearing as a 'ghost' of sorts. There is the story of the lady who frequently had vivid dreams about owning a cottage in the country – then, when touring a part of Britain she particularly liked she actually saw the property of her dreams with a 'For Sale' notice outside. Excitedly, she got in touch with the owner who admitted to her that the cottage was proving difficult to sell. Prospective buyers had been put off because they sensed it was haunted. In reply to her query about the nature of the ghost, the owner stared hard at her and replied: 'It's a woman – who has been described as looking exactly like *you*!'

So it appeared that, having visited the cottage so many times in her dream state, the woman herself had been mistaken for a ghost. Whether true or false, the story does have a kernel of fact, for some people can apparently go 'out of body', often without realising it. Our friend Sharon told me how amazed she was one evening, to see her business partner Petra outside in her garden, laughing and waving to her through the back window of her house. She wondered what on earth Petra could be doing standing in the middle of the rose-bed. But it turned out that Petra was actually several miles away, and that Sharon was witnessing one of her friend's frequent OOBEs!

I asked Petra herself for any comments. 'It seems to happen when I'm asleep. Sometimes I might think I'm dreaming,' she said. She explained that she would consciously 'turn on' when going to sleep, particularly in times of stress. 'Some years ago,' she continued, 'because of an unfortunate situation I was in, I just had to tell someone. As I went to sleep, through sheer exhaustion, I thought about a particular friend, Donna. In my dream I was talking out my problems with her. When we actually met a few days later, Donna mentioned what had been said during that conversation – which I remembered dreaming, of course. She thought I had really called in at her house, but I knew I had gone there 'out of body', though I appeared to her as solid and three-dimensional.'

Sometimes we hear how victims of accidents, sudden illness or, as patients undergoing surgery, claim to have left their physical body for a period of time, and are able to watch proceedings from above – only to regain their 'physicality' following the emergency. There are countless instances of individuals 'floating on the ceiling' while their bodies are being operated on below, often drifting out into the hospital corridor and in and out of the rooms, able to describe later what their relatives – or other people - were doing and saying in the waiting room. During my research, I came across an interesting case involving elements of both Petra's story and that of an accident victim.

Some years ago, the biologist Lyall Watson was driving with a safari party in Kenya when, suddenly losing control of his Land Rover, it skidded in the dust and twice turned over. A few moments later, he was aware of standing outside the vehicle. What he found puzzling was that he saw his unconscious self slumped inside with his passengers – and he also spotted that the body of a boy in the back had been forced through the canvas top and was hanging precariously, his head down, over a ditch. Watson knew that if the vehicle fell into it, the boy would immediately be killed. As he regained consciousness, however, Watson found himself back in his body, and was able to deal with the situation straightaway. He quickly clambered out of the Land Rover – as did everyone else – and rescued the boy moments before the vehicle actually did fall into the ditch.

Logically, you could say that not everyone is aware of experiencing these seemingly bizarre out-of-body activities. Yet maybe they are – but to a less spectacular degree. Does it really matter? Bizarre or not, they could represent some form of mechanism that helps the body or the brain – or both – to deal with, and overcome, severe trauma. And for people like Petra, being able to go OOB provides a way to help deal with problems.

28 - Psychic Protection

The presence of ghosts or spirits may not always be immediately apparent. And if they are benign, they are likely to create a pleasant atmosphere that causes no harm to anyone. On the other hand, they can inexplicably behave in a violent or hostile manner.

Near to the internationally famous Edinburgh Botanical Gardens, there was once a row of stone cottages. The attic room of Number 17, a boarding house, had a very strange atmosphere – even a weird and powerful presence. A local girl employed to clean and tidy the place on a daily basis, one day emerged from this particular room screaming hysterically. Even when she had calmed down she was unable to describe what she had encountered, but she never went in there again.

Inevitably, the reputation of Number 17 began to spread. Some students at the University challenged a colleague named Andrew Muir, a quiet, spiritual young man, to spend the night in the attic room alone 'in order to lay its spooky reputation once and for all.' The landlord readily agreed, giving him a hand-bell with strict instructions to ring it loudly should things go wrong. And everyone retired for the night.

The sleepers were rudely awakened in the early hours by a frantic ringing of the bell and also by screams of terror. Everyone rushed up to the attic room. Bursting in, they found Andrew Muir, the bell still in his hand, lying dead with a look of sheer horror on his face. He had literally been frightened to death. After that the room was locked up and never used again, Number 17 itself eventually being demolished some twenty years later.

Though thankfully most cases do not have such a disastrous outcome, the people who meddle with ghosts or spirits via the Ouija board, planchette or other methods of their own, rarely take steps to protect themselves, and put themselves at risk of at the very least, an uncomfortable and unpleasant experience. Even buyers and sellers of property today are aware of possible 'presences' lingering and do not want to encourage negative atmospheres, particularly those left by any previous owners. Such atmospheres, as we have seen, can attract a whole range of other undesirable entities over time. So if the 'feel' of a place does not seem quite right, the buyer may call on the services of a 'house-buster' (usually also a psychic or medium), who can 'clear' any negativity and also help the presence – ghost, spirit, entity or whatever – to move on.

The experienced psychic or medium, however, is well aware of the necessity of taking such precautions when encountering any reputedly haunted property, place or atmosphere. Annette John, a medium and dowser, told me: 'Never rely on hearsay. You never know *what* might be in there. Always go fully prepared.'

Some time ago I was told a very cautionary tale by Trish, a woman in her early forties, which is typical of other such stories I heard often. She and her husband were living in Bury, Lancashire when they invited friends round one evening and after a few drinks, they decided to attempt a séance using letter cards and an upturned glass.

'Nothing happened for a bit as the glass moved round the table. Then suddenly it spelt out the letters WF! Of course, we all thought it was one of us playing the fool. Then my sister, who was also there, recognised they were the initials of Will Foster, a nice lad she'd once been fond of at school. He got killed by a lorry while delivering newspapers one night, it was very sad and upsetting, as he was only fourteen at the time. Anyway, the glass continued with these other letters. It seemed as though Will was telling my sister to pack up smoking. We thought it was a great joke, a put-up job on someone's part.'

Trish's voice faltered. 'Then suddenly the glass filled up with smoke. And with none of us touching it, it was as though some invisible hand *swept* the glass off the table with tremendous force. It shot across the room and smashed to pieces against the far wall. Of course, we were terrified!'

From then on, Trish and her husband were aware that some entity was present in their house. 'It would do tricks like switching electric things on and off, make thudding noises on the floorboards upstairs, move objects about. We would lose things, only to find them in other parts of the house, days later. We somehow knew that it must have been some demon or mischievous spirit we'd let in. And according to my sister, it was not her friend Will, because he just wasn't like that.'

'What should we have done?' Trish asked, as others have queried in similar circumstances.

The answer is that if an entity has been let loose, it is already too late and the situation may need expert help to deal with it. Trish and her friends should have taken preventative measures before they held their séance; helpful actions are to repeat the Lord's Prayer together asking for protection and blessing; for each person to visualise themselves surrounded by white light. And expert help, by means of a reputable medium, should have been sought as soon as Trish and her husband realised there was an entity in the house.

The main thing is to take the supernatural and any dealings with it very seriously. Individuals under the influence of alcohol are at their most vulnerable in a situation such as this and holding a séance 'just for a giggle' is like opening your front door and inviting *anything* in. Trish, Frank and their friends were just lucky that they did not admit some really harmful, malevolent entity.

Preparations made by a psychic or medium before tackling an investigation naturally vary according to the individual. It can involve taking a long, relaxing bath the day before, followed by meditation, prayer and a good night's sleep. Although individual psychics or mediums will use the methods they find most effective for themselves they all agree that it is essential to 'go in there' feeling completely cleansed, calm and in full control of the situation. Some tell me that they take nothing of their own lives into the building; they use nothing that belongs to the householder, for this could reflect their negativity. The aim is not only to put him at his ease but also help the ghost, spirit, entity or whatever, to deal with its problems and leave.

As part of their equipment, a psychic might also take a cross or crucifix, some gemstones, oils and aromatic herbs. When I have accompanied Dilys, she has also used holy (or blessed) water, salt and smudge sticks, candles and fresh flowers left afterwards in order to help 'clear' the space and purify it after the trapped spirit has been assisted on its way.

29 - Rest in Peace

Churchyards have been the setting for many fictional ghost stories. But in reality some have been known to harbour restless spirits - one example being the Uttoxeter Road Cemetery in Derby. It is said to have an unsettling effect on people, some reporting they have sensed a presence even during days of bright sunlight. The majority of such places do possess an atmosphere of peace and well-being, however.

Although much concerned with death and resurrection, churchyards have accumulated all sorts of strange myths and superstitions down the ages. It was once considered unlucky if a person was first to be buried on the site though obviously when a long-established graveyard was filled, the next funeral procession was compelled to commit the body to so-called 'new soil' instead. Then afterwards, there was never any difficulty in getting burials performed there. Another belief was that when a person was laid to rest, they became the 'watcher of the churchyard' until such time they were relieved of the task by the interment of someone else. A slight variation in this belief was that he, or she, who was first buried in any year became 'watcher' for the full 12 months and was compelled to guard the churchyard until that time passed.

If rain fell during the funeral procession, it was considered a prelude to happiness for the deceased in the next world. In Yorkshire, if anything like a hat or a handkerchief fell into the grave, it was left there. Otherwise the person who owned it would pass away soon afterwards. To first meet someone at a graveside was said to be unlucky; and there was definite bad luck for lovers who held a secret tryst in a churchyard, terminating with a kiss - though this seems to have a certain puritanical ring about it. In Devon, if a grave was left open on a Sunday, the family would lose another member within the year. In 1864, a Suffolk woman coming out of church one Sunday saw an open grave and remarked 'There'll be somebody else wanting a grave before the week is out.' Her words came true - but the next grave to be dug was for her!

Nobody should pick or steal flowers from a grave, nor actually tread on one. A pregnant woman who does so, according to the old beliefs, will either lose her child or it will have a club-foot. Some people even in these modern days, are dubious about walking on tombstones set into the floor of a church.

The yew-tree is a stalwart in many of our churchyards. Its longevity was regarded by pagans and Christians alike, as a symbol of everlasting life. It has overseen the separation of the spirit from the body down the centuries. Our forefathers took great care in preserving the 'Funeral-tree'. To cut it down, or to burn or damage its branches is still said to be very unlucky. Formerly, at English funerals mourners would often carry yew branches, which they laid with the deceased person in the grave. A comforting thought as they represented not the end of life, but its assured continuance in the resurrection to come.

30 - Watch this Space

Why do some spirits linger on Earth while others pass on with no trouble? Why do some houses or places retain heavy emotional atmospheres while others do not? There are certain explanations that can be given, bearing in mind that ninety-nine per cent of 'spooky' stories can usually be found to have a physical rather than a psychic cause.

Buildings with strange manifestations have sometimes been built on land where there is a convergence of ley-lines (energy lines) in the ground; caves; or flowing waters deep underground which are affected by the phases of the moon: all factors which can have a negative effect on anyone living in such a building. There have been many instances where the inhabitants report feelings of debilitation and helplessness, weakness or even recurring illness as well as inexplicable depression. The expertise of a psychic investigator might be of great help in clarifying such a situation. (The ancients knew this very well – if certain plots or tracts of land were not built on over long periods of time, there was probably a very good reason.) Although not all lines of energy can be moved, the psychic or 'house buster' should be able to divert it harmlessly round the outside of the building and down the garden boundary thus dissipating any negative energies within.

By way of the ancient art of *Feng Shui*, (there are many excellent books available on the subject) he may also recommend re-positioning certain items of furniture, mirrors (especially), choosing more restful colour schemes, relocating pot-plants, and where to discreetly place crystals and gemstones in order to 'lift' dark corners and help the flow and circulation of *chi* throughout the house, promoting good feeling and sense of worth. People living in such places can also help themselves wherever possible by thinking positively.

It appears that spirits may linger and 'haunt' a property for reasons of attachment. They might have hated the place and still feel trapped there; or they might have loved the dwelling so much they are reluctant to leave. Often the spirit is concerned about what changes the next owner might want to make and may be opposed to such changes. On some occasions it does not realize it has actually died, and wonders what these strange new people are doing in '*my* house.'

Other stories concern spirits which seem to have delayed their journey into eternity in order to carry out 'unfinished business'. In 1910 the author Charles Kent wrote about some poachers in Croxton, Norfolk who killed a gamekeeper and hid his body on their cart among the dead hares and rabbits. They made their way towards Thetford, where there was an old chalk-pit; but as they lifted the body from the cart in order to bury it, the corpse roused itself and pronounced a curse, vowed to haunt the men for the rest of their lives. Hastily the murderers 'finished him off proper' then buried him in the chalk-pit, where it was later claimed that a hearse, coffin and bearers were seen regularly in the dead of night.

Emerging from the chalk-pit, the phantom cortege proceeded a short distance down the road, then turned and retraced its steps to the place where the gamekeeper was buried. Charles Kent added that for several decades before he had placed the story on record, young people from the neighbourhood regularly went to the chalk-pit at night to witness the phantom event for themselves.

Ipstones churchyard in Staffordshire is a very haunted place. One of the most mysterious entities lingering there takes the form of a disembodied voice which, in a foreign tongue, whispers into the ears of many surprised visitors. Near the village is what is known as Horsley's Stone, said to be frequented by the spirit of a small bird, thought to be an omen of good luck for anyone psychic enough to see it.

Staring from a window in a room of the former Berwick Arms at Atcham Bridge in Shropshire is the ghost of Jack Mytton, the 'Mad Squire'. Proudly wearing a riding coat and high boots, he is often seen looking out over the River Severn, which still flows under the bridge over which his funeral cortege passed on its way from Shrewsbury in 1834. It was here, at the Berwick Arms that his coffin rested overnight before being taken the next morning on to Halston for the burial service. It was also at the Berwick Arms that the local people were able to pay their last respects to their hard-drinking, hard-riding, generously eccentric 'Mad Squire' who had died at the age of thirty-eight.

The former Berwick Arms at Atcham is now a first-class hotel, the Mytton and Mermaid, which celebrates Mad Jack's memory not only by renaming itself in his honour, but by calling the former tap-room 'Mad Jack's Bar' – here were preserved various memorabilia of this notorious local character.

One William Hughes, many years ago recounted to Miss C. S. Burne, author of *Folklore of Shropshire* his father's recollection of crossing the Long Mynde at twilight. On his way to the small village of Ratlinghope, he encountered a Victorian funeral procession which passed him at great speed. He was forced to stand aside to allow the horse-drawn hearse to pass, with a large number of people formally dressed, all following hurriedly behind. On his arrival at Ratlinghope, Mr Hughes, Senior, made enquiries about what he had encountered. He was surprised to learn that it was the so-called Phantom Funeral, which had been seen by many other people over time, usually at dusk. Whose funeral it was, and any further details, were completely unknown to the local population.

It was once thought unlucky for anyone to come face-to-face with a funeral - though one wonders whether this also applies to someone encountering a phantom funeral?

We live our lives entirely within a framework of ghostly activity and magical superstition, good and bad – in fact, sometimes both at the same time. Dilys says she walks under ladders (which brings bad luck) – but that if she crosses her fingers as she does so, the disaster will be averted. Crazy or what? So many contrary superstitions remain as links with the pagan world. When somebody sneezes, for instance, the response is 'Bless you!' This is one of the most well-known superstitions – another being that if someone bites their tongue, they have recently told a lie. Covering one's mouth when yawning is another protective gesture, all these lingering from times when life was very hazardous. The deadly plague was so easily passed on. Evil spirits might enter or leave the body when someone yawned or sneezed. There is far more resting on these simple gestures than good manners!

For me it has to be a question of 'Watch this Space'. So many more cryptic stories still await exploration and explanation by a Ghost Reporter, whether or not the supernatural can be proved responsible. Meanwhile, the ghosts continue to go on their way; the phantom Victorian funeral, with its mourners, continues time after time to hurry towards that unknown grave.

Contact Details

Enquiries & orders
Phone: 01298 212386

E-mail
anecdotespublishing@btinternet.com

Or go to
www.lulu.com
and search 'Paul Gater'